POSITIVE
Gun Dogs
Clicker Training for Sporting Breeds

A
Karen Pryor
Clicker
Book

POSITIVE
Gun Dogs
Clicker Training for Sporting Breeds

Jim Barry, CPDT, CDBC

Mary Emmen, MA

Susan Smith, CTC, CPDT, CDBC

Positive Gun Dogs
Clicker Training for Sporting Breeds

Published by Sunshine Books, Inc.
47 River Street, Suite 3
Waltham, MA 02453
781-398-0754
www.clickertraining.com

ISBN 1-890948-33-0
Printed in the United States of America

Library of Congress Number: 2006939797

9   8   7   6   5   4   3   2   1

This book is available at quantity discounts for multiple-copy
purchases. For information call 1-800-47-CLICK.

Contents

So you have a new gun dog. Congratulations! You are not alone; sporting breeds are among the most popular dogs in America. Almost 200,000 Labrador and golden retrievers were registered with the American Kennel Club in 2005, along with more than 50,000 pointers, setters, spaniels, and other hunting breeds.

There's good reason for the popularity of these breeds. Hunting is one of the oldest activities shared by dogs and humans. Because success in the hunt requires close cooperation, effective communication, and a deep and trusting relationship, dogs that have been bred for this purpose are hardy, intelligent, highly trainable, and remarkable in the deep bonds that they form with their people.

If you are reading this book, you have probably already decided that you want to experience the joy and satisfaction that comes from bringing out the best in your dog's hunting and retrieving talents. Whether you are looking for a hunting companion, plan to participate in field sports, or simply want to see your dog do the things he was bred to do, you have a rewarding journey ahead of you.

Like us, you have probably looked through several books on training hunting dogs. Maybe you've watched training at breed clubs or seen a professional trainer work. If so, you may have been dismayed (as we were) to discover that most training methods for gun dogs rely on the use of force and pain—ear pinches, wedging dowels between the dog's toes, and shock collars. And you may have wondered if these punishing techniques are really the best way to train your dog. (See box: What Is "Force Fetch"?)

What Is "Force Fetch"?

"Force fetch" is a training method that relies on negative reinforcement to train a dog to take, hold, and release an object. It is the foundation for "force" or "pressure" training. This approach to training is based on the philosophy that retrieving is a demanding skill; it's not necessarily in the dog's comfort zone. Therefore, the dog must learn to tolerate discomfort at each stage in the training process.

To teach force fetch, the trainer starts with an appropriate retrieving object, usually a dummy or a paint roller. (Some trainers restrain the dog on a table during the process.) The trainer then applies a stimulus to the dog, usually by pinching the ear or by inserting a dowel between the toes and using a cord to compress them. When the dog opens his mouth, the trainer inserts the retrieving object into the dog's mouth and stops applying the stimulus. The dog is then required to hold the object for longer periods of time or to move forward to take the object before the stimulus stops. Eventually, the trainer moves the object to the floor and the dog learns it can cause the painful stimulus to end by picking the object up on the command "fetch." The command is then generalized to other objects and the distance is extended so that the dog must run out and return with the item it has retrieved.

(continues)

What Is "Force Fetch"? *(continued)*

Evan Graham, one of the most articulate proponents of this training method, observes in *Smartworks for Retrievers* (Rush Creek Press, 2002) that the objectives of force fetching are to teach appropriate mouth habits, including hold and delivery, to ensure compliance with the "retrieve" command under demanding conditions in the field, and to impart momentum.

Force fetch is followed by such exercises as "stick fetch" (applying a stimulus with a stick as the dog leaves on a retrieve), "force to pile" (using an ear pinch or a stimulus from an electronic collar as a dog leaves to pick up a dummy from a distant pile), and "water force" (the same process when doing a water retrieve). The result, according to Graham, is "an animal far more driven, with much more resolve to overcome obstacles and distance and distractions." As trainers John and Amy Dahl put it in *The 10-Minute Retriever* (Willow Press, 2001), force training is "a matter of teaching the dog that nothing that happens as a result of going on a retrieve will be as bad as the consequences of not going."

The force fetch technique uses goals and methods opposite to those of positive trainers. Positive trainers use *reinforcers*, rather than negative stimuli, to teach and maintain behavior. In positive training, when punishment is necessary to decrease unwanted behavior, a gentle reminder is used or a reinforcer is withheld to improve compliance. Thus, positive training seeks to motivate a dog to overcome obstacles through the expectation of a reinforcer rather than through anticipation of a negative consequence for not complying with the trainer's wishes. (The method of teaching a dog to retrieve by using positive reinforcement is described in Chapter 6.)

We think not. In our experience as trainers and dog lovers, we have seen dogs trained to very high standards with positive, humane methods. We have used these methods with our own dogs and many of our colleagues have trained effective hunting dogs by focusing on reinforcement rather than punishment. We also know that world-class trainers like Bob and Marian Bailey have used positive training methods with thousands of animals, from more than 120 species, to achieve extraordinary results. (Our favorite of their accomplishments is the cat that Bob trained to hold a half-hour sit-stay in Los Angeles International Airport!)

We believe strongly in the benefits and effectiveness of positive training, hence this book. In online discussions with hundreds of gun dog owners, we found that a real need exists for a book that compiles information on a positive approach to training the basic hunting skills. Almost without exception, new members of the PositiveGunDogs Yahoo Group discussion list have asked for information on books that could help them to learn positive methods for training their dogs. Until now, they have had to rely primarily on traditional training books, modifying them if they wished to use positive methods. So we saw real value in writing a book that would summarize the insights from members of that list and provide resources that new gun dog owners could consult in order to use positive methods from the beginning.

Our goals in writing this book are modest. Because it is one of the first of its kind, we hope this book serves to establish a foundation for further development of positive gun dog training. Our intended readers are both new gun dog owners who want either a solid hunting companion or to compete in hunt tests, and more experienced hunters who want to learn a positive method of training. (See Appendix II for a description of hunt tests and other field sports.)

We are confident that positive methods can be effective at advanced levels of hunting dog field trials; however, there are as yet no field champions to our knowledge that have been trained using exclusively positive methods. There are several reasons for this. Positive training for dogs has become popular only in the past decade. Most practitioners are pet dog trainers or participants in other dog sports such as agility and competitive obedience. Interest in training gun dogs with positive methods has been limited to date, although that interest is growing. Furthermore, field trialing a dog is expensive, both in terms of time and cost. Because traditional methods have proven to be successful, there is little incentive to risk using as yet unproven techniques. We believe, however, based on the experience of the Baileys and others, that the day will come when positively trained dogs will compete at the highest levels in field sports. They already achieve top honors in other dog sports such as competitive obedience and agility, and we are confident that it is only a matter of time before dogs trained with positive methods will be top competitors in field trials as well.

At the outset, we must acknowledge that we are not professional gun dog trainers. There are many highly successful pros, and even more accomplished amateurs, who have developed excellent, systematic training programs. (See Appendix I for a list of some of these trainers' books and videos.) We have drawn on some of their programs (with appropriate acknowledgment) and have adapted their ideas to positive training methods. In some cases, we have tested these positive approaches fully, either with our own dogs or in our training classes. In others, which we point out, the methods are untested with hunting dogs but are based on extensive experience in other areas of dog training or in the training of other species. In a sense, the information presented here is not new; what is revolutionary is the use of positive training to develop effective gun dogs and faithful, lifelong companions.

Plan of the Book

We intend this as a resource book, not as a training "system." Thus we have organized the chapters to provide information ranging from the basics of learning theory to advanced drills. We begin by describing the fundamentals of how animals learn. We then proceed to general techniques for training using positive methods. Because it is so important to proceed systematically and keep track of progress, we include a chapter on criteria setting and record keeping.

Next we provide information on training some of the basic commands your dog will need: heeling (walking at your side), coming in on command, sitting, stopping, and staying in position. These behaviors form the foundation for more advanced training. In subsequent chapters, we discuss specific goals for gun dog training, devoting a chapter to equipment, selection of training areas, and conditioning to gun and bird. Finally, we give suggestions for training the key skills for gun dogs: retrieving, hunting systematically, pointing, and flushing. Appendixes provide information on additional training resources (Appendix I) and field sports (Appendix II).

Acknowledgments

The authors would like to acknowledge the contributions of many extraordinary trainers to the development of dog training and of the hunting breeds. We are particularly indebted to the Baileys, Ian Dunbar, Jean Donaldson, Pat Miller, Karen Pryor, Kathy Sdao, and others who pioneered and popularized positive training, and to Steve Rafe, who was one of the first to employ positive methods in training field dogs. And although we don't endorse all of their methods, we should note the contributions of Rex Carr, whose programs form the basis for most retriever trainers today, as well as Evan Graham, Mike Lardy, and other trainers who have developed highly structured and effective training systems. And we would also like to thank the more than 600 members of the PostiveGunDogs discussion list for sharing their experiences and approaches so generously. It is our fervent hope that the cadre of positive gun dog trainers will expand from hundreds to thousands. We are proud to have been part of this remarkable and dedicated group.

Chapter 1

Basic Learning Theory

A basic understanding of learning theory is essential if you want to be an effective and efficient dog trainer, and have fun in the process. Most dog training today is based on tradition and lore that has been passed down from trainer to trainer in a sort of informal apprenticeship system (see box: A Brief History of Dog Training). If you were to ask the average gun dog trainer to explain learning theory, he or she would not be able to do so and might even scoff at the idea of needing to understand such a thing. Despite their lack of familiarity with learning theory, though, these trainers are applying the laws of learning—whether they know it or not—when they train their dog and the dog learns the behavior. Many trainers are also probably not aware that they may be wasting valuable time and energy on techniques that do not teach the dog anything and may actually be impeding the learning process. We are in no way suggesting that these trainers have nothing to offer—on the contrary, they have a great deal of knowledge and experience to pass on. However, we can't help but wonder how much greater they'd be if they knew their learning theory!

One problem with traditional models of training is that they defy what's known as "Morgan's Canon of Parsimony." At the end of the nineteenth century, Lloyd Morgan addressed the problem of attributing complex reasons to simple behaviors. Pamela Reid quotes Morgan's Canon in her book *Excel-erated Learning* (James & Kenneth Publishers, 1996): "In no case is an animal activity to be interpreted in terms of higher psychological processes, if it can be fairly interpreted in terms of processes which stand lower in the scale of psychological evolution and development."

Too often we assume there are complex causes motivating our dogs when, in fact, the dog simply does not understand what we want her to do. Let's say we've taught our dog to retrieve a dummy in the backyard. We've worked diligently and done some fairly advanced work such as blind retrieves. We then take the dog to the field and ask our dog to do a very simple retrieve from only about 2 or 3 yards away. Our dog does not retrieve the dummy. We might attribute our dog's inaction to stubbornness, but in reality what's happening is that the behavior we have trained our dog to do has not been generalized to situations outside the backyard. The dog simply doesn't understand what she's supposed to do.

Let's think about this scenario in terms of Morgan's Canon of Parsimony. Stubbornness, which we might originally think is what's behind the dog's behavior, involves a lot more than the dog just not knowing what to do. Stubbornness implies resistance, malice, forethought, and a whole host of other complex processes, whereas not being trained is very simple. We, as trainers, need to get away from the belief that our dogs are deliberately defying us. In general, dogs will perform the trained behavior if they know what is expected of them and how to do it, and the motivation is sufficient.

Increasing numbers of animal trainers are beginning to put learning theory to good use. Many trainers working with wild animals in zoos and animal parks have been using these techniques for years; only within the last two decades have trainers of domestic animals such as dogs and horses begun to use these methods seriously. There are some exceptions, such as the Baileys (Bob and Marion), who have trained many hundreds of animals for commercial and military use over the last 50-plus years using the principles of operant conditioning.

A Brief History of Dog Training

Why bother with learning theory? The answer is that learning theory helps to dispel the myths that have plagued dog training and have led to the abuse of dogs when trying to change their behavior. A little history may help to demonstrate the value of learning theory as it relates to dog training. The following is condensed from Mary Burch and Jon Bailey's *How Dogs Learn* (MacMillan, 1999).

People have been training dogs for thousands of years, but the modern history of dog training begins with our own sporting breeds. In the nineteenth century, British sportsmen exhibited their well-trained sporting dogs; this practice spread to the United States. Training for obedience began in America in the 1930s. Dog training first became a profession after World War II, when returning soldiers taught others how they had trained war dogs. Not surprisingly, the methods used tended to be harsh. Two trainers in particular, Konrad Most and William Koehler, advocated the use of choke collars and other punishment devices. Their approaches had been effective for protection dogs, and Koehler's fame as principal animal trainer for Walt Disney helped popularize his techniques.

During the 1960s, several books suggested gentler methods, but it was not until the 1980s that learning theory became an integral part of dog training. Dr. Ian Dunbar, a veterinary behaviorist, began teaching seminars in which he applied learning theory to help resolve problem behaviors. In 1984, Karen Pryor, a marine mammal trainer, published her groundbreaking book *Don't Shoot the Dog,* which forged an important link between science and training. In 1994, Dunbar and his colleagues founded the Association of Pet Dog Trainers (APDT), an organization dedicated to promoting dog-friendly training through education.

Bob Bailey told us in a personal communication that his colleague Kellar Breland used positive training methods on two field dogs in the 1940s, but that he was unable to interest gun dog trainers in his techniques. He—and later Bob—turned his attention to commercial animal training, where he had great success. In the 1950s and 1960s, the training of gun dogs in the United States became systematic, and a number of professional gun dog trainers set up shop. Prominent among these was Rex Carr, who developed the basic drills used by most retriever trainers today. In addition, the invention of the electronic collar, which can deliver a shock to a dog at a distance from the trainer, provided a new tool that gun dog trainers could use in their programs. Trainers were quick to institute these devices in their training programs, and almost all professional gun dog trainers in the United States now use them.

While the training of pet dogs and dogs that compete in obedience, agility, and other sports has relied increasingly on learning theory, the training of gun dogs has remained largely the domain of professional trainers who rely on tradition and electronic collars. We would argue that the success achieved by most gun dog trainers has come not because they understand how dogs learn, but in spite of their lack of systematic understanding. And the popularity of their aversive-based methods has led to the continuation of myths that get in the way of effective training for hunting dogs—such as that pointing dogs should never be trained to sit, or that dogs must be punished in order to learn to retrieve in difficult conditions. It is our hope that sound scientific methods can eventually replace these myths.

Learning theory is based on proven science, with laws governing its principles. All types of learning can be understood through principles of learning theory. According to these principles, there are certain laws of nature that apply to all physically and mentally healthy animals. Further, all animals, from the lowliest cockroach to the most sophisticated human, learn in the same way. Once you've read this book and understand some basic learning theory, you will not only know how to train your dog, but also your spouse and your boss! Just to clarify, when we talk about animals as a group, we are including humans in that group; humans learn the same way dogs do.

Some excellent books are available that explain learning theory in a clear and easy-to-understand manner. We've already mentioned two of our favorites. One is *Excel-erated Learning*, by Pamela J. Reid, Ph.D. Reid's book is a must for any serious dog trainer. The book is written specifically for dog trainers, is organized in a way that allows it to be used as a reference book, and is extremely easy to read and understand. (See Appendix I for more information.) Another helpful book is *How Dogs Learn*, by Mary R. Burch, Ph.D. and Jon S. Bailey, Ph.D. Because there are already so many good sources of information about learning theory, we will not go into great detail on the subject. However, in this chapter, we provide an overview of the basic principles you should know before getting started with training your dog; more sophisticated learning concepts are addressed throughout the book.

What Is Learning?

Learning is a change in behavior, based on experience, that continues over time. The behavior change doesn't necessarily happen immediately; it may not be demonstrated until there is a need. This is called latent learning—the learning has occurred, but the behavior has not yet demonstrably changed. Learning may also be latent when a dog is not physically able to perform the behavior; for instance, a puppy may learn that she is supposed to eliminate outdoors, but may not be physically mature enough to control herself.

How Animals Learn

The ability to learn is genetic; learning itself is not genetic. Essentially, animals learn through experience. The ability to learn and adapt is what allows us to survive in this dangerous world. The psychologist named Edward L. Thorndike boiled it all down in his very simple Law of Effect: "The principle that, in any given situation, the probability of a behavior occurring is a function of the consequences that behavior has had in that situation in the past. An abbreviated form says that behavior is a function of its consequences" (Behavior Analysis Glossary, University of South Florida, www.coedu.usf.edu/abaglossary/glossarymain.asp?AID=5&ID=2194).

Operant Conditioning

Thorndike's statement brings us to the foundation of training, which is called the four quadrants of operant conditioning. According to learning theory, an action can have two types of consequences: reinforcement or punishment. These consequences can occur in two different ways: they can be added or taken away. A reinforcement increases the likelihood of a behavior. A punishment decreases the likelihood of a behavior. The paradigm is illustrated in Figure 1.1.

Although the quadrant may look complicated at first glance, it is really quite simple. The main things to remember when trying to determine which quadrant is at work on the dog are:

- "Positive" and "negative" are used the same way here as they are in mathematics: When you use positive reinforcement or positive punishment, you are adding something. When you use negative reinforcement or negative punishment, you are removing something.

- Reinforcement leads to a behavior increase; punishment leads to a behavior decrease.

- You, the trainer, do not determine whether something is reinforcing or punishing—the dog does! You may consider something reinforcing, but if the behavior does not increase, then it is not reinforcing to the dog. If the behavior decreases, it is actually punishing to the dog. We can make educated guesses as to what might be reinforcing or punishing, but the proof is in the behavior.

1.1 Operant Conditioning Quadrants

Action Stimulus	Add	Remove
Desired	Positive Reinforcement (R+)	Negative Punishment (P–)
Undesired	Negative Reinforcement (R–)	Positive Punishment (P+)

Following are examples of the four quadrants (these examples assume you get the results you are hoping for):

- R+: You give your dog the "sit" cue, your dog sits, and you give her a treat. (Giving the treat should make the sit-on-cue happen more often.)

- R–: You give your dog the "sit" cue, your dog doesn't sit so you give a leash pop, your dog sits, and you release the leash. (The R– is the release of the leash and should make the sit-on-cue happen more often.)

- P+: You give your dog the "down" cue, your dog doesn't down, so you step on the leash, forcing the dog into a down. (The P+ is the physical force that requires the dog to "down" and should decrease the dog's standing or sitting behavior.)

- P–: Your dog jumps on you so you put her in her crate for 30 seconds then release her. (You cannot have P– without R+, so in this example the removal of a stimulating environment is the P– and should decrease the jumping behavior; the R+ is being allowed out of the crate into a more stimulating environment.)

You can think of an aversive as something the dog will avoid. Using an aversive is: the onset of a stimulus decreases one behavior, and the termination of the same stimulus increases another behavior.

Positive reinforcement trainers try to use primarily the R+/P– quadrants of the model. We feel that these quadrants do the least harm and promote active learning and problem-solving in dogs. (Some trainers who are primarily positive in their approach may use P+ or R– as a last resort, but they do so rarely.)

Operant Conditioning

Operant conditioning (also called instrumental conditioning or Skinnerian conditioning after scientist B.F. Skinner, who systematized it in the lab) means that the animal realizes that its behavior has consequences and chooses to act according to the consequences. In operant conditioning, animals have control over their response to an event.

The sequence of events (in scientific terms, the contingency) in operant conditioning is: when A happens *and I do B*, then C will happen. For example, when I hear thunder, if I roll up my car windows, the inside of my car will not get soaked if it starts raining. I could opt not to roll up my windows and, in that case, I've made the choice to take the chance that either it won't rain or the inside of my car will be soaked. For the most part, we use operant conditioning techniques when training a dog. We address these techniques in more detail throughout the book, particularly in Chapter 2.

Classical Conditioning

Classical conditioning means that an association is made between two events. The first event reliably predicts the second event. Some common examples are: a flash of lightning reliably predicts a clap of thunder; the ringing of the doorbell reliably predicts a visitor. There are other, more subtle associations as well: a particular song evokes a memory of an important time or event; the smell of a certain perfume evokes the memory of a particular person. Generally, with a classically conditioned behavior, the animal has no control over its response to the event, and the response is usually physiological in some way—perhaps the heart beats faster, or the pupils dilate.

The principles of classical conditioning were established by the Russian scientist Ivan Pavlov while he was studying the digestive system of dogs. He noticed that when the person who fed the dogs appeared, the dogs began salivating. Pavlov then began investigating this phenomenon, which led to our understanding of what we call classical conditioning (sometimes called Pavlovian conditioning or associative learning). The contingency in classical conditioning is that Event A predicts Event B. (There is no intervening behavior choice as there is in operant conditioning; classical conditioning is involuntary.)

Although there are many ways classical conditioning can be useful when working with problem behaviors such as fear and aggression, the importance of classical conditioning for dog trainers is that we can take a neutral stimulus and, by associating it with something the dog wants (usually food, but not necessarily), give it meaning. A popular way to do this is to use a clicker, a small plastic box with a metal tab that makes a clicking sound when pushed. If we repeatedly pair the sound of the clicker with food, the click becomes meaningful to the dog, telling him food is coming. We can then use the clicker—which has become a conditioned (or secondary) reinforcer—to signal a reinforcer to the dog when we cannot immediately deliver a primary reinforcer, such as food. We discuss developing and maintaining this association much more thoroughly in Chapter 2, which deals with using clicker training techniques as a basis for gun dog training.

The Link Between Classical and Operant Conditioning

Although we discuss classical and operant conditioning as if they were two separate things, they both happen at the same time. You cannot learn something operantly without also creating a classical association and vice versa. What we, as trainers, need to know is that classically learned behaviors will always trump operantly learned behaviors if push comes to shove. As Bob Bailey says in his training classes, "Pavlov is always sitting on your shoulder."

Extinction

Extinction is an important element of learning. Extinction occurs when a behavior is neither reinforced nor punished, and so it eventually goes away, or extinguishes. It is important to remember that animals do what works. If an animal continues to perform certain behaviors, there is undoubtedly a payoff somewhere. An excellent way to deal with certain undesirable behaviors is simply to extin-

guish them. Behaviors such as pawing for attention, barking to be let in, counter surfing, and so on, are excellent candidates for extinction. A caution for the gun dog arena: do not try to extinguish an undesired behavior, such as chasing animals or birds, that is inherently reinforcing. Because this behavior brings its own reinforcement, it will not extinguish. Another caveat is that "extinction" is a behavioral term and does not mean that the behavior is gone forever; under the right circumstances, it will reappear.

External Inhibition and Disinhibition

Figure 1.2, which is adapted from Jean Donaldson's course at the San Francisco SPCA Academy for dog trainers, shows normal learning patterns. Two of these areas are vital to dog trainers: the external inhibition and disinhibition patterns.

External inhibition happens when an animal shows a steady increase in learning (understanding) a behavior, then suddenly seems to have forgotten everything it learned. This is normal and happens all the time; humans refer to it as a block. When this happens, it's best to end the session, give the dog a break from training, and try again the next day or the day after. When you start your new training session, the dog should be back to normal and may even be ahead of the game. Instead of getting frustrated, realize that this happens when the learning is coming together in the dog's head and is starting to make sense.

The opposite of external inhibition is disinhibition. Disinhibition occurs during extinction and is also called "spontaneous recovery." Spontaneous recovery takes the form of a renewed effort to make what has previously worked work again. Suppose you've made up your mind to ignore your dog when she scratches on the door to be let in. This tactic appears to be working well; it has been quite some time since your dog has scratched on the door. Then, all of a sudden, she scratches on the door! This is spontaneous recovery. Don't get upset, give in, or punish the dog. Just ignore the behavior; if it is not reinforced, it will go away.

1.2 Normal Learning Patterns

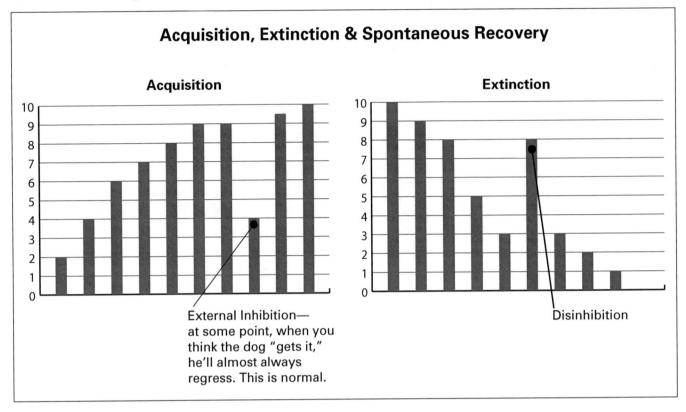

Four Stages of Learning

There are four stages of learning. When training a new behavior, you must address each of these stages before you can consider the behavior trained. The four stages are:

- **Acquisition:** The process of learning the new behavior

- **Fluency:** Perfecting the behavior and having the behavior become automatic

- **Generalization:** The process of learning to perform the behavior under a different condition or in a different environment

- **Maintenance:** Practicing the behavior on an ongoing basis to ensure the behavior continues

Discrimination and Generalization

Although all animals learn in the same ways, each species has its peculiarities. One of the biggest differences between dogs and humans is in their abilities to discriminate and generalize.

Discrimination means being able to tell the difference between situations. The better you are at discriminating, the more subtle the differences you can discriminate. Dogs are excellent discriminators, whereas humans are not as good. Dogs know who will let them jump up on them and who won't; they know that it's okay to get on the couch when Mom is home but not to get on the couch when Dad is home; they know that Dad is more likely to play rough games than Mom; they know that when your finger twitches on the trigger, there will be a bird to retrieve. In training, they know when you have food in your hand and when you don't, when you're using a dummy or a live bird, and they undoubtedly know when you're serious about training and when you're not really in the mood!

Generalization means that you can take a concept from one situation to another and still understand it. Humans are excellent generalizers. But because dogs are such good discriminators, they are not great generalizers. They can discriminate between one set of circumstances and another but, if there are differences, then they do not usually relate the behavior learned in one set of circumstances to a new one. This is why it is so important to start at the beginning again when you add something new to a behavior. For instance, you train your dog to roll over in your living room, then you take her to your father-in-law's house to show her off, and she acts like she's never heard the cue before! And, in fact, she does not understand what you want—you must retrain the behavior in the new location. Once you have trained the behavior in enough different situations, she'll realize that the cue prompts the physical act, regardless of the circumstances.

Another common generalization issue is with housetraining. Your dog is well housetrained in your house, but you take her to a friend's house and she promptly eliminates. She has not learned that it is being inside a building that is the cue for not eliminating and must be taught this in a variety of settings before it will click for her.

Discrimination and generalization are crucial concepts for dog trainers to understand. When a trainer does not grasp these concepts, he or she may become frustrated and embarrassed and treat the dog harshly—blaming the dog when the real problem is a lack of training.

These concepts are particularly important for gun dog trainers, who must realize that there are profound differences between training in the yard and in the field. There are also differences between training and testing, between structured competitions and hunting, and between waterfowl and upland game hunting. Each situation must be thoroughly trained. Trying to overcome the dog's inability to generalize by resorting to forceful methods is likely to be less effective than systematic training, and can be abusive as well.

Habituation

Habituation allows us to ignore unimportant stimuli in the environment. If we had to pay attention to every noise, every smell, and every movement that took place, we would be in sensory overload! Habituation is the means by which we filter out what is not relevant to our well-being. We learn to ignore things that happen continuously or on a regular basis, but pay attention to things that happen only occasionally. For instance, we may not notice the noises our refrigerator makes because we are used to hearing them, but when we go to a house we've never been to before, we notice the refrigerator noises. That's because we have habituated to our refrigerator's noises but not to an unfamiliar refrigerator's noises.

Habituation is of particular relevance to gun dog trainers. When our dogs first go out into the field, they are on sensory overload. They are not yet used to the sights, sounds, and smells, and genetically they are particularly attuned to them.

The environment in which we train is called the stimulus package. There are ways to deal with the stimulus package, which are addressed in Chapter 2.

Sensitization and Desensitization

Sensitization occurs when an animal is exposed to something and becomes increasingly sensitive to it. An example is the vacuum cleaner. Dogs often become sensitized to the vacuum cleaner's combination of noise and movement, and can become quite aroused and even aggressive when they are exposed to one.

Desensitization is the opposite of sensitization and is usually accomplished through gradual, low-level exposure to the item the dog is sensitized to. The key to desensitization is to keep the dog at a comfort level at all times; if you go too fast, you risk sensitizing the dog, rather than desensitizing her.

Flooding

Flooding is repeatedly exposing the dog to something she is sensitized to, keeping her above her comfort level until she habituates to it. This is not recommended because it can easily backfire and sensitize the dog even more. Sometimes trainers use this technique to acclimate dogs to loud noises such as gunshots. This can be very dangerous, and we strongly recommend desensitization instead.

Overshadowing and Blocking

Overshadowing occurs when you give two cues at the same time and the dog hones in on the more prominent cue. So, let's say you are training your dog to heel and, in so doing, you give your verbal cue and the dog heels. What you don't realize is that when you give the verbal cue, you also move your left foot because you are ready to take a step. If the dog is cueing into the foot movement rather than the verbal cue, when you move your left foot without giving your cue, the dog believes she is supposed to heel. Because you really want her to stay in the sit position, you think she is breaking her sit-stay. Conversely, one day you may give the verbal "heel" cue without moving your foot and your dog will not heel.

Blocking occurs when a new cue gives the dog no new information. In training, this usually happens when we're trying to change an existing cue or add a new cue. For instance, if you trained your dog to sit using a lure, your dog probably has a hand signal cue for "sit" that mimics the movement of the hand holding the lure. Now you want to add a verbal cue. If you say "sit" at the same time that you give the hand signal, you are blocking the verbal cue, because the verbal cue gives the dog no new or important information. We'll discuss the proper way to add a new cue in Chapter 4.

Conditioned Emotional Response

A conditioned emotional response (CER) is a classically conditioned response to a specific circumstance. Animals develop CERs all the time and to almost everything they encounter. Here are some of the obvious things to which our dogs have developed CERs: leashes, other dogs, particular car routes, the electric can opener, and the sound of the refrigerator door opening. Most CERs are not of major importance one way or the other; however, others can be problematic. Be aware that you can change CERs through classical conditioning if they are a problem.

You can also create a CER, which is exactly what you are doing when you first expose your dog to birds. All good bird dog trainers do their best to create a good CER between the dog and the bird; the last thing we want is for the dog to dislike birds! If, for some reason, your dog has developed an unpleasant CER to birds, you can reverse this by pairing the bird with good things such as food or play.

Premack Principle

The Premack Principle (named for psychologist David Premack) states that in order to get a lower probability behavior (something the dog is unlikely to do), use a higher probability behavior (something the dog is likely to do). In other words, use something the dog wants to do to get her to do something she doesn't want to do. For instance, she must sit politely at the door before she can go out, she must be steady before she can retrieve the bird, and so on. This is an important principle when dealing with animals (including human animals) living in a social situation. We must train impulse control in our dogs and children from an early age; Premack is the ideal solution for impulse control. In order to get what you want, you must be polite and patient! We mention Premack frequently throughout this book because it is such an important tool in training.

Aversive Training

There have been many studies done on the use of aversives. Using aversive training is applying the R– and P+ half of the operant conditioning quadrant. We do not claim that aversive training does not work, because it does; however, there are many good reasons not to use aversives if you can avoid them. The biggest problem with aversive training is that you run the risk of creating a dog that suppresses *all* behavior, not just the behavior you are training her to suppress.

We will explain what happens when you use R– and P+ to train your dog, using the "sit" command as an example. Most traditional training is based on avoidance. We'll assume the dog has been taught the basics of sit by being pushed into position. This is called placement (or, in current politically correct jargon, modeling). Suppose that we are now going to work on fluency. We give the "sit" cue and, when the dog does not sit, we give a pop on the leash, which causes the collar to tighten around the dog's neck and the dog sits. If we look at this sequence from a learning theory viewpoint, here's what happened: Because the dog did not respond to the "sit" command, the handler popped the leash. This created either discomfort or pain (P+), and the dog changed position to avoid the discomfort; because the dog's choice was to sit, the discomfort ended because the trainer loosened the collar (R–). Repeated enough times, this technique will teach the dog to sit on cue. Remember, P+ means you've added something to decrease behavior. In this case, you've added the leash pop to decrease the standing behavior. R– means you remove something to increase behavior. In this case, you removed the discomfort of the collar to increase the sitting behavior.

Remember: you cannot apply a negative without also applying the corresponding positive. In other words, you cannot have R– without P+, and you cannot have P– without R+. The problem with R– and P+ is that they can suppress all behavior, not just the behavior you are targeting. If the dog does not understand why she is being punished (which she undoubtedly does not in the beginning), she will suppress all behaviors because she doesn't know which one will cause the discomfort. This is a key difference between dogs that have been trained using aversives (such as force fetch, as described in the introduction) and those that have been trained using positive reinforcement. A positively trained dog will offer behaviors until he finds the one that will earn a reinforcement; the dog that has been trained with aversives will more frequently avoid offering behaviors out of fear of punishment.

The only exception we make to using R– and P+ in dog training is for snake avoidance training, because of safety issues. We have no doubt that a dog could be trained to avoid snakes through R+ methods; however, the time and dedication this would take makes it highly unlikely to happen with the average dog. There are different methods out there for snake avoidance training, but they all use R–, and we feel that electronic collar training is the most reliable. If you do choose to use an electronic collar to train snake avoidance, take your dog to a person who specializes in this type of training and watch the trainer work before subjecting your dog to this highly painful and potentially damaging training. Make sure the trainer knows the principles of avoidance training and has excellent timing and criteria standards (a predetermined desired response from the dog). Snake aversion training is an unpleasant experience; we've observed people laughing at the dogs as they react to the shock, perhaps using laughter to mask their discomfort. If you train in an area that has poisonous snakes, you must address the dilemma of whether to use aversive training.

Shaping Through Successive Approximation

Shaping through successive approximation simply means that you are shaping a behavior by taking baby steps toward the goal behavior. By setting realistic, achievable criteria, you will make steady progress toward the goal and will reach it more quickly than if you set goals that are too difficult for your dog to attain.

Throughout this book you will see statements such as: "If your dog does not perform, you have moved ahead too quickly; go back a few steps and start again." What this means is that you have set an unattainable goal for your dog. If your dog always achieves the goal, you are probably setting your criteria too low; if your dog frequently does not achieve the goal, you are setting your criteria too high. Aim for at least an 80:20 ratio of success to failure. Your dog should succeed 80% of the time.

Chapter 3 deals with criteria setting, record keeping, and measuring behavior. If you master these techniques, you should be well on your way to understanding how to set achievable criteria. Once you can do that, your training will move along very quickly.

Conclusion

Some of the more important learning theory principles apply to gun dog training. As we said at the beginning of this chapter, we cover actual training techniques (which, of course, follow the learning theory principles) in more detail in Chapter 4 through Chapter 8. Additional learning concepts are addressed throughout the book. We highly recommend you invest in Dr. Pamela Reid's book *Excelerated Learning*, or Mary Burch and Jon Bailey's book *How Dogs Learn*, and bone up on your learning theory—either will stand you in good stead during training.

Chapter 2
Positive Reinforcement and Clicker Training

What Is Clicker Training?

A clicker trainer is a trainer who uses a clicker as a secondary reinforcer to train animals. As mentioned in Chapter 1, the clicker is classically conditioned to the primary reinforcer. A primary reinforcer is anything the dog intrinsically wants—food, retrieving, and so on. Most clicker trainers use primarily R+ and some P–; they rarely use any P+ or R–. The authors of this book want to be efficient trainers who use as little P+ and R– as possible. Our goal is to have happy dogs that enjoy life and are well trained. We feel that our methods work well in achieving this goal. We use a variety of methods: we use the clicker when appropriate, we lure when appropriate, and we try to think outside the box to solve the problems that arise while training positively. If you want to train your gun dog to a high level, we believe the use of the clicker will be extremely beneficial. This chapter discusses various training concepts, including the use of a clicker (or other instrument) as a secondary reinforcer.

As we mentioned in the introduction, some of the methods we recommend have not been tested specifically with hunting dogs. Positive reinforcement training is based on a concept different from traditional training. In traditional training, you wait for the dog to make a mistake and you correct her; with positive reinforcement (R+), you wait for the dog to succeed and reinforce her. This is not to say that traditional trainers don't encourage and help their dogs to get the behavior right from the start, because of course they do! However, the way we change behavior differs significantly. Because of this difference in philosophy, there is also a difference in the way you will approach the training. R+ train-

ing requires more planning before you get to the actual training. When you approach training from the clicker philosophy, you must do everything you can to communicate what you want so the dog will succeed from the start. Remember that every time your dog performs a behavior, whether desired or undesired, she is practicing that behavior; if you are trying to eliminate corrections from your training program, you must also eliminate undesired behavior. The way to do that is to plan ahead.

Clicker training is based on solid science. To help you make the transition to this type of training, this book includes plans and record-keeping models for you to study and learn from. We also explain some of the pitfalls that you might encounter and offer suggestions for avoiding them.

Terminology

We use the terms "trial" and "set" to describe repetitions of a behavior. A trial is one repetition of a behavior, for instance, one sit from the time it is cued until it is either reinforced or the dog does not respond to the cue. A set is a series of trials. It might help to think of trials and sets as reps and sets in weight lifting; they are exactly the same principle.

C/T means click then treat.

How Does One Get Started Using a Clicker?

The first thing to do is decide what you are going to use as your secondary reinforcer. You can use pretty much anything, but it should be convenient and easily handled. Some people use a clicker; some people use whistles. If you plan on using a whistle to give cues to your dog, we do not recommend using it as a secondary reinforcer as it may confuse your dog. There are some remote clicker collars on the market now, so clickers are more viable for field work; however, the reports we've received indicate that the timing of the remote clickers leaves something to be desired. Some people use a "bridge word" rather than a mechanical sound. This has an advantage—you can't leave it at home—but also may be more difficult for the dog to hear and less precise than the clicker. We condition both a clicker and a bridge word but use the clicker for introducing new commands.

There are some basic rules to follow when using a secondary reinforcer. (These assume you're using a clicker.)

- Every time you click, follow the click with the primary reinforcer. If you don't, you will weaken the association and may eventually lose it altogether.

- Click as the dog is performing the desired behavior or within ½ second of the performance. If you wait any longer, you are clicking a different behavior. Dogs are smart, and they usually learn in spite of us, but the better we are at our timing, the quicker they learn. Additionally, if you regularly click a behavior that is not the behavior you are looking for, you run the risk of training a "superstitious behavior." This means the dog thinks the behavior she's being clicked for is part of the behavior you are training. Depending on what the superstitious behavior is, it may become a problem down the road. As Bob Bailey says in his seminars, "You get what you click, not what you want!"

- Although the secondary reinforcer is often called a "bridge" because it allows a time gap between the performance of the behavior and the delivery of the primary reinforcer, the sooner you can deliver the primary reinforcer, the better. Reinforcers are called primary and secondary for a reason! When you first start out, you should be delivering the primary reinforcer almost immediately. Once you've built a strong association, you can then allow more time between the secondary and the primary, but you should always deliver the primary as soon as possible.

- Only click once! Sometimes when new clicker trainers get excited, they repeatedly click. This gives the dog no useful information and violates the rule that you must deliver a primary for every secondary.

- Do not use the secondary reinforcer as a keep-going signal. In Chapter 4, we address the concept of a keep-going signal, which is controversial among positive trainers. While such a signal has valuable uses, if you have set proper criteria and trained the dog accordingly, she will rarely need it. And if you do use a keep-going signal, it must be different from your click or other reward marker.

- Finally, remember that the click ends the behavior. Once the dog hears the secondary reinforcer, she may stop what she's doing and come to collect her primary reinforcer. This is perfectly okay; you are training for a specific behavior and once the dog has performed it, she has earned her reinforcement.

Now that you know the rules, here's how to get started. You should have the appropriate basic equipment, which includes the following:

- The secondary reinforcer

- A bait bag (carpenter aprons or fanny packs work very well)

- A target stick (a collapsible pointer, a wooden kitchen spoon, a pen, or a ¼-inch dowel with the ends painted black work just as well as an expensive, professional target stick)

- Primary reinforcers (you should always have food with you, but you may also want toys—it will depend on the training session)

2.1 Essential Equipment

Clicker and whistle

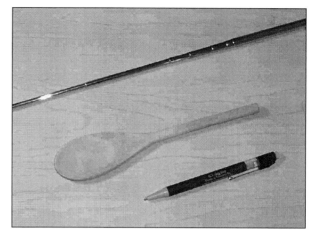

Target stick

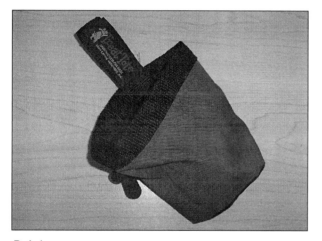

Bait bag

Treat & Train

A new device that has great potential is the Treat & Train. This product was invented by Dr. Sophia Yin for remote training. The Treat & Train is a remote treat delivery system that was distributed commercially by Sharper Image. At this writing, Sharper Image reportedly is discontinuing sales, but the devices are still available from online auction sites, and we understand that the manufacturer is looking for an alternative distributor. It may help you when you start working distance behaviors and may help transition from the yard to the field at fairly close distance. Eventually, the retrieve itself will be the motivation to work, but the Treat &

Train is an intriguing invention we encourage you to explore. For more information on this system, find the Yahoo Group discussion list by searching for "treatntrain" at http://groups.yahoo.com.

Begin clicker training by "charging" your dog. The purpose of this exercise is to introduce your dog to the clicker and create a positive association with its sound: a click means a treat is coming. Regardless of what your dog is doing, you click and treat (C/T). When charging your dog, you should be very close so you can immediately give the dog the treat. Also, be careful not to click while the dog is doing a specific behavior, since you are only charging, not training. Also do not click an undesired behavior; even though you're charging, the dog is being reinforced. After you've done 15 to 20 C/Ts, wait until your dog is facing away from you, then C/T. If your dog turns back to you to get the treat, she's charged. If she ignores it, do another 15 to 20 C/Ts. Once the dog is charged, she'll remain charged unless you click without treating often enough that she loses the association, or you stop C/T for a long enough period of time that she loses the association. You have to charge your dog only once; you do not need to charge her at the beginning of each training session.

Now that you've charged your dog and have the equipment you need, you can begin formal training. If you've never clicker trained your dog, we recommend you start at the beginning, even if your dog already knows the behavior. This will give you an opportunity to practice your technique and will also strengthen the dog's association and allow her to understand that this is the way training is going to happen from now on.

For more information on efficient training, see Chapter 3: Criteria Setting and Record Keeping. Also, if you can, take a course from a clicker trainer. You can use the trainer search at www.apdt.com to find R+ trainers in your area. They will not all be clicker trainers, but you should be able to find someone who can work with you. Another excellent resource to find a clicker trainer (as well as good information) is www.clickersolutions.com. We've listed other resources in Appendix I.

The Mindset

Good R+ training requires thinking differently than you have in the past. Once you develop the correct thinking patterns, these new principles will fall into place and make sense to you. Another benefit of practicing correct thinking patterns is that you will develop the ability to analyze most problems on the spot; some may take a little more thought and perhaps some brainstorming with a friend, but most will be obvious.

The Four Elements of Training

Training consists of four basic elements. These are: timing, motivation, criteria, and rate of reinforcement (ROR). In order to train a behavior, all four elements must be present.

Timing

Although timing seems self-explanatory, good timing requires practice, good observational skills, and a specific, defined criterion. Bob Bailey tells his students, "Training is a mechanical skill." What he means is, if you want to learn to be a good trainer, you can; it simply takes understanding the concepts and practicing the skill sets. (Appendix I includes Internet links to various exercises you can use to practice your timing.)

Almost every behavior has a corresponding precursor behavior. A precursor is something that precedes and predicts something else. For example, lightning always precedes thunder, and it also always predicts thunder, so lightning is a precursor for thunder.

This concept applies in dog training. If you practice watching dogs, you will become familiar with canine body language. If you watch your own dog, you will become familiar with her particular signals. If you watch your dog do the same behavior over and over, you will soon recognize the precursor behavior to the behavior you are watching for. This means you will be able to anticipate the behavior, and your timing will be impeccable! As with any training, the more structured you are in your observations, the quicker and better you will become at knowing your dog's precursor behaviors.

Once you've learned to recognize certain precursors, you can anticipate what your dog's next behavior will be and, if it's an undesired behavior, you can stop it before it happens, thus preventing her from practicing undesired behaviors. If it's a precursor to a desired behavior, you will be ready to reinforce with your secondary reinforcer the instant it happens. Almost all behaviors have a precursor. It may be very obvious, as with hackles and ears, or it may be very subtle, involving just a slight change in posture. A good example of a precursor is when your dog is in a sit-stay and is about to go into a down, she'll put one of her front feet out. If you see that happen, you can give a quick "ah!" or another "stay" signal to prevent her from breaking her stay.

Motivation

As with timing, motivation appears to be simple; however, it is actually quite complex. Any number of things can motivate a dog; the trick is to find motivators that you can use in training. Food is one of the most efficient motivators around, especially at the beginning stages of training a behavior. When you start taking your dog out into the field, finding good motivators will become harder. This is one of the challenges of training.

Three principal motivators are "hardwired" into the dog. Food is the first, because it is basic to survival. Another is sex (yes, sex!), which is basic to continuation of the canine species. This is rarely a practical motivator for dog training, although Bob Bailey did use it for training marine mammals. The third is play, specifically the kind of play that emulates the dog's predatory behavior—finding, stalking, chasing, tugging, shaking, and yes, retrieving! For gun dogs, some of the behaviors we are trying to train are themselves motivators.

The problem with using play as a motivator is that it takes time. If we had to stop and let our dogs tug on their toys after each trial, a set could take forever. However, used judiciously, play can be a powerful motivator. We often use a "happy bumper"—a dummy tossed just for fun—as a reinforcer in training our gun dogs.

For some dogs, praise and petting can be motivators, but not all dogs find these rewards to be powerful and, in comparison to the hardwired reinforcer, they are weak. But, used carefully in a program of varied reinforcements, praise and petting can be helpful.

That leaves food. Many trainers think their dogs are not motivated by food; however, that is unlikely. All healthy animals are motivated by food. You can build food's motivating qualities by using it a lot and using it consistently. In addition, by using very small food treats, you can get lots of "reps" into your training and build stronger responses. If you are not in the habit of training with food, even if

your dog has been taught the basics it's a good idea to go back to the beginning and reinforce liberally with food in low-distraction areas. You can then gradually increase the distractions while maintaining the value of the food. (We discuss the "stimulus package" and how to deal with it later in this chapter.)

Before moving on from the topic of motivators, we want to mention the tendency to blame everything but ourselves when our training doesn't go the way we want it to. Use the least valuable motivator the dog will work for and save the big guns for difficult environmental challenges. It's easy to get caught up in searching for a more motivating treat if your dog doesn't perform for the treat you are offering. There are times when this is perfectly valid; however, treat value can become a red herring. The value of the treat may not be the issue at all; more likely, criteria and rate of reinforcement are the real culprits.

Criteria

Criteria, or a criterion, is the specific behavior (or even a piece of a behavior) you are currently training. If you don't know what your criterion is, your timing will be off because you don't know what to reinforce! Further, you will confuse the dog because he can't possibly know what you want if you don't know what you want. Be precise in your criteria-setting. Know exactly what you are looking for and don't fudge in either direction! We will discuss when to increase your criteria in Chapter 3, which covers measuring behavior and record keeping.

Rate of reinforcement

Rate of reinforcement (ROR) is exactly what it sounds like: how often the dog is being reinforced for performing a given behavior within a given period of time. ROR will vary according to the behavior, the stage of training of the behavior, and the dog.

In our experience, ROR is the number one thing that trainers neglect. Yet it is probably the single most important aspect of training. ROR will tell you if you have good timing, if your reinforcer is motivating, and if you have set good criteria. If you do not have a high ROR, you need to reevaluate at least one of the other three elements of training.

The Link Between Criteria and ROR

Criteria and ROR are linked and cannot be separated. When you have low criteria you will have high ROR; when you raise your criteria your ROR will go down. This is a natural ebb and flow. The trick is to set your criteria so that, within a few trials, your ROR will come back to where it was when you raised your criteria—10 trials should be more than enough. If your ROR doesn't come back up this quickly, you've raised your criteria too high. There will be occasions when you must raise your criteria higher than you would like, but these should be the exception rather than the rule.

Some people believe that it takes longer to train a dog using R+ methods; we propose that those trainers are not paying attention to their ROR! If you set good criteria (which is determined through ROR), it shouldn't take more than a few trials for the dog to learn the behavior well enough that you can raise the criteria again. In the early stages of training, a few trials happen in one minute or less. Later, when the behaviors are more complex and cover more distance, it will take longer to raise the criteria, but not as long as it would if your dog were making errors along the way. Again, the key is to plan ahead so your dog never makes errors. If you do this, the training advances very quickly.

Reinforcement Schedules

Reinforcement schedules are also a crucial aspect of training. It is human nature to want to eliminate reinforcement as quickly as possible; the trick is in eliminating it in the right way. In R+ training, we generally stay on a 100% reinforcement schedule until the behavior is exactly the way we want it. However, in a sense we are reducing the reinforcer every time we raise our criteria. Each time you raise your criteria, you stop reinforcing the previous level of performance and only reinforce the new level.

The exception to this principle is training distance and duration behaviors. When you set your new criteria, occasionally reinforce for a shorter distance or duration, so the dog succeeds at an easy task. This keeps the dog engaged. Remember that if a behavior is not reinforced, it will extinguish; easy trials keep the behavior from extinguishing.

Something else to remember about reinforcement schedules is that a variable reinforcement schedule (VRS) can cause positive variations in performance. Using VRS, if you don't reinforce the dog for a performance you've reinforced her for previously, her next performance is likely to be stronger in some way. It's as if the dog is putting emphasis on her performance to show you that she did what you wanted. Then, when you get something more, reinforce it, and you have achieved a new performance level.

There are several kinds of reinforcement schedules, but we will address only the schedules that pertain to gun dog training.

Continuous reinforcement schedule

When using a continuous reinforcement schedule (CRF), you reinforce every successful trial. It is always best to use a CRF when training a new behavior. The responses will not necessarily be spectacular, but they will happen.

Variable reinforcement schedule

When using a variable reinforcement schedule (VRF), you reinforce only certain behaviors. A VRF will create variability of behavior, which allows you to refine the behavior; VRF also strengthens behavior. Within a VRF you can have: fixed ratio (FR), which might be every third repetition; variable ratio (VR), which might be on average every third repetition; random ratio (RR), which has no pattern; fixed interval (FI), which might be every 30 seconds; variable interval (VI), which might be on average every 30 seconds; or random interval (RI), which has no pattern.

Differential schedules

When using differential *rate* schedules, you reinforce a *rate* of behavior rather than a *level* of behavior. When you want to reduce latency (speed of response), use a differential rate schedule. Within a differential rate schedule you can use a differential reinforcement of high rates of behavior (DRH), or differential reinforcement of low rates of behavior (DRL).

You can also use differential *type* schedules, which means you are reinforcing a *level* or *quality* of behavior. For example, if you want a straight sit, you determine what "straight" means in terms of criteria and reinforce only those sits that meet or exceed the criteria. Within a differential type schedule you have:

- Differential reinforcement of other behavior (DRO), which could include rewarding a sit on approach rather than jumping up

- Differential reinforcement of incompatible behavior (DRI), which could include retrieving a tennis ball when the doorbell rings instead of barking

- Differential reinforcement of excellent behavior (DRE), which is rewarding an especially good performance

Duration reinforcement schedules

Finally, we have duration reinforcement schedules. Within the category of duration schedules we have fixed duration (FD), variable duration (VD), and random duration (RD).

The schedules that will have the most impact on gun dog training are the CRF, DRH, and DRE. There may be occasion to use differential reinforcement of other behaviors or differential reinforcement of an incompatible behavior, but only if you are attempting to eliminate an undesired behavior such as munching on the bird.

The Stimulus Package

The stimulus package is of crucial importance to gun dog training. The stimulus package is, in a word, the environment. Anything that will take your dog's attention away from you is part of the stimulus package. There are two ways to deal with the stimulus package: satiation and motivation. We usually use a combination of the two.

Satiation occurs when you allow your dog to get her fill of the environment before trying to train her. Depending on the dog and how often she gets out into the field, the amount of time needed for satiation will vary. If you take your dog out just once a

Inherently Reinforcing Behavior

One of the pluses in gun dog training is that many of the behaviors we are trying to train are themselves rewarding, because they are part of the dog's "hardwired" predatory cycle. This is true for many aspects of hunting, pointing, flushing, and retrieving. So when you are working with your gun dog, it's important to assess whether these inherently reinforcing behaviors are sufficient to maintain or improve the skills you are training, or whether you will need to supplement them with other rewards. How will you know? The dog's behavior will tell you!

There is a minus side to these behaviors. Because they are so attractive, these behaviors can cause a dog to go awry in search of a reinforcement when you don't want her to. To mitigate this, it's important to introduce distractions systematically and also to have a solid method for interrupting your dog, such as a reliable recall or whistle stop, so that you can regain control.

month, it will take her longer to be satiated than if you go out daily. Most gun dog trainers instinctively use satiation; they let their dogs run, sniff, pee, and so on before beginning the training session.

Deprivation means you have withheld a form of motivator to later make it more motivating. For example, if you do not feed your dog for 12 hours before training, she will be hungry and more motivated by food.

The motivator, of course, must be something more interesting than the stimulus package. For most of our dogs, it is hard to find something more motivating than the open field. However, with work and time, you will be able to motivate your dog in the field. If using food, you will probably need to use something of very high value; you will also need to train your dog to take food in the field.

Satiation and Motivation in Practice

The way Jim handles his training sessions in the field is by first airing his black Lab, Toby, on a long lead. When Jim has studied the area carefully and is confident that it is safe from coyotes, skunks, stray fish hooks, and so on, he lets Toby off lead to explore while he sets up the equipment. After, they do a little bit of obedience, and Jim tosses a dummy or two. Then Jim always starts off with a couple of marks (retrieves of dummies) to keep Toby's adrenaline flowing. They then work on whatever is on the agenda for that day—lining, casting, extending the distance of marks, or working with higher cover, for example. (These drills are covered in Chapters 6 and 7 on retrieving.) Jim tries to keep the session short and focused, if possible, and follows it with a couple of "happy bumpers" for Toby to chase. He then puts the equipment away, except for the dummy launcher (see Figure 5.8 in Chapter 5). When he's reloaded the truck, he pops off a couple of dummies for Toby, with at least one in the water if conditions permit. Toby really loves to get those dummies. When Jim puts Toby back in his crate in the truck, he also tries to have on hand a "good dog" reward, such as a great big marrow bone.

The obvious motivator for most gun dogs is the prey. Finding and/or retrieving the bird is a highly potent reinforcer. However, you must do it right and train your dog that she can do these things only if she's done everything else that you want her to do. You can use the Premack Principle creatively and liberally when working in the field.

Targeting

Targeting can be useful in directional training. Targeting means training your dog to touch an object on command. You simply hold the object close to your dog and wait for the dog to bump it with his nose. Then click and treat. After a few repetitions, the dog will begin to offer the behavior, and you can add a cue. Once you've trained your dog to target an object, you can then use that object to move the dog around or to increase distance. We explain how to use a target stick for sending the dog away from you—called "lining" or "go out"—later on. Some trainers use a target for almost every behavior they train, so feel free to experiment beyond the exercises we introduce.

Length of Training Sessions

It is important to limit training sessions. Dogs do not have long attention spans and need to break fairly often. In the early stages of training a behavior, plan on 5- to 10-minute sessions. Once you're out in the field, it is not convenient to train for 10 minutes and then go home, so plan on doing a short training session, then let your dog have a 10- to 15-minute break where she can explore and play and you can log your session. Then do another short session, give the dog a break, and so on. It is best to stop training before you or your dog gets frustrated. If you're having trouble with a particular behavior, stop training, analyze the situation, and revisit it later.

On a related note is the phenomenon called "icing the dog." This means that you're having an average or maybe even a lackluster performance from your dog so you decide to quit training for the day. The next day you begin your training session and your dog performs like a champ! This is part of the external inhibition process we discussed in Chapter 1. Humans also do this—we have a problem that we've been mulling over all day, we go home and sleep, and the next day the solution appears so obvious we can't figure out why we didn't think of it before! This is a normal phase of the learning process, and one of the big reasons short training sessions are more productive.

Motivators

Motivators are a crucial part of training. All training involves motivators, whether it's avoidance or acquisition. R+ uses acquisition of something the dog wants as a motivator.

What to use as a motivator

You can use access to the outside, to a person, to a toy, and so on, as motivators, but they are generally not as efficient as food. Even though you can use anything the dog wants as a motivator, food is extremely efficient, especially in the early stages of training; it's small (easy to carry and your dog won't get full), quickly dispensed (keeps the ROR high), and highly motivating. Store-bought treats are generally not as motivating as hot dogs and are usually more expensive. If you've done a lot of food-based training prior to going into the field, you should be able to continue using it; however, you may need to raise the level of the food and use roast beef, prime rib fat, garlic roasted chicken, stinky cheese, tuna, liverwurst, or other tempting foods. Once you're out in the field, you can still use food for close-in work, but you'll eventually want to transition to another, more powerful motivator—hopefully hunting and retrieving!

How much food to use

If you're using junk food for treats or working with a puppy, don't allow the treats to comprise more than 20% of your dog's daily caloric intake. If you're training an adult dog and using high-quality food such as beef or chicken, you can increase that percentage significantly.

Use the smallest treats possible. If you're using regular-sized hot dogs, quarter them lengthwise, then chop them into pea-sized pieces. You should get at least 75 treats out of one hot dog! You don't want to overdo the treats, because they will become less motivating as the dog gets full. If you're working with small dogs such as American cocker spaniels, you may want to make your treats even smaller.

The Mindset Revisited

Now that you've read this chapter, it's time to start working on the way you think about training. When you're training and your dog does not perform the way you expect, instead of continuing what you're doing, becoming frustrated, or correcting the dog, stop and think to yourself, "Why isn't the dog performing this behavior?" Remember, there are only four things that could be the problem: timing, motivation, criteria, or rate of reinforcement. It *has* to be one of those four, or any of them in combination.

You Want Me to Do What?

We can explain the simplest things by first thinking of the four elements of training. Sue was teaching an obedience class in a room that has a stage. She was standing on the stage and asked her dog, Jimmy Joe (who was on the main floor), to sit. Jimmy Joe was looking right at her and paying attention but did not sit. Because Sue is in the habit of thinking about why her dog doesn't perform when asked, she immediately realized that she had never asked her dog to sit while she was standing 2 feet above him. That particular criterion had never been addressed! Because Jimmy Joe has an excellent sit, we call this a generalizing issue; in reality it is a criteria issue, as are all generalizing issues. As soon as she recognized the problem, Sue reduced the criteria by giving the hand signal for sit, which is more noticeable to Jimmy Joe. When he saw the hand signal, Jimmy Joe immediately sat!

2.2 Wick

Wick, in the blind, is showing rapt attention to the field. This is a dog "marking." The duck being returned is a cripple that gave Wick a real chase in the water. Wick persisted and grabbed the duck so as not to be bitten. This took place at a hunt test in Connecticut when Wick was eight years old. He is still trained entirely without aversives except for putting him up, or threatening to, when he understands but chooses not to—not always an easy call, but I think after all our work together I can tell. Wick also has AKC UD, TD, AX, and AXJ titles, all trained positively. His brother and his brother's daughter also have JH titles, all trained without aversives.

(Photo by Tom Reese)

Chapter 3

Criteria Setting and Record Keeping

To train efficiently and well, the trainer should set quickly achievable criteria. This involves breaking down a behavior into very small increments and training each increment to a desired level of fluency. In dog training, the rule of thumb for fluency before raising criteria is an 80% compliance rate. If you are setting good criteria, your dog should learn most increments of behavior within one set, or five to ten trials.

Record keeping helps you to know when you have reached an 80% compliance rate. It also keeps you on track; if you are logging your sessions in writing, you will always know where you've been and where you need to go. Record keeping also allows you to gather data you might need for statistical or other purposes.

Equipment

The following is a list of equipment you will need to keep good records of your training:

- Three-ring binder, ½-inch to 1-inch thick (one binder per dog unless you're training a lot of dogs, in which case you can get a thicker binder)

- Page dividers

- Three-ring binder plastic pencil holder (to hold pencils, clickers, stop watch, voice recorder, whistle, and other small equipment)

- Voice recorder (optional)

- Treat holder (The hardware departments of many stores have inexpensive, clear-plastic boxes with removable dividers. You can count out your treats in advance and put them in the divided compartments. This will save you a lot of time during your training session, and you can carry it with you without worrying about the treats falling into another section.)

- Pens, pencils

- Stopwatch

Clicker Basics

Summarized here are the important, basic tenets of clicker training, many of which we have covered earlier.

Deliver your treat as quickly as possible after the secondary reinforcer. We tend to think of the primary and secondary reinforcers as distinct events; however, reinforcement is a process and there is a proven relationship between the speed of learning and the speed of delivery of the primary reinforcer. Additionally, every behavior that happens between the click and the delivery of the primary is being reinforced. Because you are working in the field, you'll be doing a great deal of distance work. Reserve slow delivery of primary reinforcers for distance behaviors. Don't weaken the power of your secondary reinforcer unless you must, and don't reinforce any peripheral behaviors you may not want unless you have to.

When possible, deliver the treat only when the dog is in the position you want and, if at all possible, in position for the next piece of the behavior you are training. For example, suppose you are training your dog to pick up a bird and then return to you. If you are still working fairly close to the dog, click for picking up the bird, but reinforce when the dog has begun turning toward you. This will train the dog to turn toward you, which is the next step of your training process, anyway! As Bob Bailey says in his training classes, "Click for behavior, treat for position."

Record Keeping Specifics

Why keep records? We keep records for several reasons:

- Keeping track of where you are. Many trainers (including the authors, on occasion) fall into the trap of "lazy training." This means we train a behavior that the dog has already learned. If you keep a training log and refer to it prior to your training session, you will know exactly what you need to work on during the current session. This increases your efficiency and also turns out a better-trained dog.

- Stumbling blocks. It can be difficult to analyze problems when you are in the midst of them. By keeping a training log, you can go back, review sessions, and pinpoint where you got off track.

- Data gathering. Individual trainers may or may not care about keeping statistics; however, if they keep records of their training sessions, they can compile data at some point in the future. If you are training for others, that data can be very useful.

Basic Rules for Setting and Raising Criteria

Do not raise criteria until the dog performs the specified behavior 80% of the time the cue is presented. With behaviors such as the recall, raise the criteria only when the dog performs the behavior 100% of the time the cue is presented.

Your goal is to set a new criterion that is attainable within five to ten trials. Set only one new criterion at a time. For example, don't increase both distance and duration in the same set.

When making a big jump in the criterion (e.g., going from the house to the field), lower all other criteria except the one you are currently working on. For instance, if you are working on duration for stay, you want to decrease distance, distraction, and owner orientation. This principle is one of the more important ones and you will see it applied throughout this book.

How to Evaluate Behavior

For serious trainers—competitors, professional trainers, or even serious amateurs—efficiency is important. The best way to be efficient—to know where you've been and where you need to go—is to keep a training log. A training log provides a means of evaluating your skills. Are you setting criteria increases efficiently? Are you moving ahead instead of training a behavior the dog already knows? Are you inadvertently adding more elements to the behavior than you realize? What time of day gets the best results?

A lot of trainers dread the thought of keeping a training record, but if you use an efficient form (or series of forms), it takes only a few moments to keep track of your training sessions, and it will save you time and headaches. You can streamline the process by purchasing a pocket voice recorder. Using the recorder, simply state the current criteria and how your dog performs; then, once you're home, you can transfer the data into your training logs.

Here are sample logs with explanations of how to use them. At the end of the book are some blank logs you can print out and use.

3.1 Sample Training Log

Training Log (Behavior Being Trained)

Log # _____   Date _____

Time _____   Treat _____

Session Goal: _____

Beginning Measurement: _____

End Measurement: _____

Comments: _____

_____

Summary of Session: _____

Distance _____

Duration _____

Distraction _____

Orientation _____

Location _____

Understanding the Training Log

- Behavior entered next to "Training Log" describes final goal behavior, for example, "competition sit in heel position."

- Enter the "Log # = session number" value on the corresponding measurement log (see below). File the measurement log directly behind the Training Log for easy reference.

- Enter the date.

- Enter the time of day.

- "Session Goal" describes what you want to accomplish during the training session. Set the goal at the end of the previous session, for example, "= butt at 90% angle to final heel position." Setting your next session goal at the end of the current session will help keep you on track and will also help you avoid the "lazy trainer syndrome."

- Record the treat used.

- "Beginning Measurements" and "End Measurements" are the measurements you take at the beginning of the session and at the end of your previous session. You measure the same behavior at the beginning of your next session to see if it has improved, regressed, or stayed the same. If it has regressed, you need to work that criteria some more.

- Enter comments in the "Comments about session" field to capture information that is not already on the form.

- The Summary indicates where you are with each of the basic components that need to be trained—distance, duration, distraction, and handler orientation. This section of the form will help you remember how to set up the next training session so that you are not raising more than one criterion at a time.

3.2 Sample Worksheet

Rate of Behavior (compliance)

Session Log #: _____   Total Treats: _____

Treats Left: _____   Rate: _____

Latency (speed of compliance)

Session Log #: _____

___ ___ ___ ___ ___ ___ ___ ___

___ ___ ___ ___ ___ ___ ___ ___

Total: _____ / _____ = _____

Speed (overall speed of behavior)

Session Log #: _____

Time Allotted: _____

Total Treats: _____   Treats Dispensed: _____

The Worksheet has three different measurements on it; you'll use the Rate of Behavior most often.

Rate of Behavior (Compliance)

Rate of behavior is used to measure compliance, that is, whether the dog understands what you want him to do. The standard measure for compliance is 80%. If the dog performs the behavior 80% of the time the stimulus is presented, you can assume he understands the behavior.

To measure compliance:

- Count out a set number of treats—usually five or ten.

- Decide how long you are willing to wait after presenting the stimulus. (We tell handlers to count to 30; however, we usually wait until we feel we've lost the dog.) You can work on speed of compliance (latency) at a later training session.

- Present the stimulus and wait for compliance.

- If the dog complies, C/T.

- If the dog does not comply, set a treat aside.

- At the end of the set, count the number of treats you have set aside and figure the rate of compliance (treats left ÷ total treats used = % of treats left). Subtract that figure from 100% to get the rate of compliance. For example, suppose you start with 10 treats and have 3 treats left at the end of the set. Divide 3 by 10 = .3 or 30%. Subtract 30 from 100 and you get a 70% compliance rate.

Understanding the Rate of Behavior Log

> **Rate of Behavior** (compliance)
>
> Session Log #: _____   Total Treats: _____
>
> Treats Left: _____   Rate: _____

- "Session Log #" is the session number on the training log that corresponds with this measurement.

- "Total Treats" is the total number of treats you started with, usually five or ten.

- "Treats Left" is the number of treats left at the end of the session. You will have treats left only if the dog did not perform the cued behavior within the time allotted.

- "Rate" is the rate of compliance. Divide the number of treats left by the number of treats started with, then subtract that number from 100 and that will be your rate of compliance.

- If compliance is 80% or better, you can raise your criteria.

Latency (Speed of Compliance)

Latency is part of training fluency. Once your dog knows what you want him to do, you need to get him to respond quickly to the cue. This is called measuring latency.

To measure latency:

- Develop a counting rhythm. Practice this rhythm so that it is natural to you before you start working with the dog. Use the same rhythm at all times, as this is how you measure elapsed time without using a watch.

- Count out a set number of treats (usually ten).

- Decide the amount of time you will allow for compliance.

- Give the cue, then begin counting.

- Once the dog begins to comply, stop counting and record that number. Be sure you know what behavior you will consider the beginning of compliance. It should be the same for each trial.

- Add the numbers together, then divide by the total number of treats dispensed.

- This will give you the average time (per your counting rhythm) that it takes for your dog to comply.

- Latency for each set should be less than it was in the previous set, assuming the criteria remain the same.

Understanding the Latency Log

> **Latency** (speed of compliance)
>
> Session Log #: _____
>
> ___ ___ ___ ___ ___ ___ ___ ___
>
> ___ ___ ___ ___ ___ ___ ___ ___
>
> Total: _____ / _____ = _____

- "Session Log #" is the session number on the training log that corresponds to this measurement.

- Each time you give a cue, you count in your counting rhythm until the behavior starts and enter that number in the blank provided. (This is where a voice recorder comes in handy!)

- Add all the numbers, then divide by the number of treats dispensed. That number is your average latency.

Speed

Speed means the overall time it took the behavior to occur from the time the cue was delivered until the behavior was completed. You generally use this value in proofing the final behavior.

To measure speed:

- Set a timer for a set period of time (30 seconds, 45 seconds, and so on).

- Count out significantly more treats than you expect to use (for example, if you expect the dog to sit 20 times in 30 seconds, count out 30 to 40 treats).

- Give the cue and reinforce the behavior as quickly as you can.

- At the end of the time, count how many treats you have left and subtract that number from the total treats. That will give you the speed of the dog's response.

If you are not organized, the count will be skewed and will not accurately measure the dog's speed.

Understanding the Speed Log

Speed (overall speed of behavior)
Session Log #: _____
Time Allotted: _____
Total Treats: _____   Treats Dispensed: _____

- "Session Log #" is the session number on the training log that corresponds to this measurement.

- "Time Allotted" is how long you have spent on this set of trials.

- "Total Treats" is the total number you started with and should be more than the number of behaviors you expect the dog to perform.

- After you finish the set, count the number of treats left and subtract that figure from the total treats. That will tell you how many treats were dispensed and how many times the dog performed the behavior in a set period of time.

Acquiring Stimulus Control

Karen Pryor, who popularized positive training in her book *Don't Shoot the Dog*, asserts that the goal of training is stimulus control. According to Pryor, stimulus control occurs when the following four conditions are present:

- The behavior always occurs immediately upon presentation of the conditioned stimulus (compliance and latency—for example, the dog sits when told to).

- The behavior never occurs in the absence of the stimulus (for example, during a training or work session, the dog never sits spontaneously).

- The behavior never occurs in response to some other stimulus (for example, if you say, "Lie down," the dog does not offer the sit instead).

- No other behavior occurs in response to this stimulus (for example, when you say "sit," the dog does not respond by lying down or leaping up and licking your face).

The following statement is crucial to gaining stimulus control: *If the behavior is strong enough to be given spontaneously, then you can reinforce it only when you cue it, without fear that it will extinguish.* Remember that "extinguish" is a behavioral term. Once a behavior has been reinforced, it will never really be extinguished; under the right circumstances it will come back. So if your dog has been reinforced enough that she is spontaneously offering behaviors, you can safely stop reinforcing an uncued behavior without worrying about extinguishing. It should happen on cue, and that is what you want to reinforce.

To gain stimulus control, *never* reinforce a behavior unless you have given the dog the cue to perform that behavior. Once you've established your cue, stop reinforcing unrequested behaviors.

You may have already started on your obedience, but it is so crucial to good field work that we decided to include a chapter on the behaviors needed in the field. Any obedience your dog learns will make for a better dog, but there are a few specific behaviors that need to be trained to a fairly high level for field work: sit, stay, target, heel, recall, and leave it (dropping an object on command).

Techniques Used

There are different ways to train behaviors. This is a quick overview of the methods we will talk about in this chapter.

Luring

Luring is using food or another object, such as a toy, to get the dog into the position you want. There's an old axiom in horse training: "Control the head and you control the body." This is the basic philosophy of luring, and it is often the quickest way to get the desired behavior.

Capturing

Capturing is waiting for the behavior you want and reinforcing it. You can capture anything the dog does naturally: sitting, howling, pricking her ears, and so on. Capturing can take longer than luring, but if you have a dog that simply doesn't want to do something, it's often the best way to get the behavior.

Shaping

You can use shaping with both luring and capturing. Shaping is taking a piece of the behavior you want and reinforcing it until the dog is reliably offering it, then asking for a little more. A good example of shaping is with a down. Some dogs resist going into a down position and it can sometimes be difficult to lure a down. However, by using shaping techniques, you can quickly get the behavior. Suppose your dog is in a sitting position and you want her to go all the way down. Using a lure, you'll first click for the dog lowering her head to follow the treat. Then click for a little bend in one of the front elbows or hunched shoulders, then for putting one of her front feet out in the beginnings of a down, and so on. In fact, we are almost always shaping, since we rarely get exactly the behavior we want first time out.

Schedules of Reinforcement

We addressed reinforcement schedules earlier in the book but want to touch on them again in this chapter. We recommend you think about the reinforcement schedule you plan to use before you start to train.

For most basic training, you'll probably use one of two techniques: a continuous reinforcement schedule until you reach the final target behavior; or continuous reinforcement until the dog is at 80%, switching to a variable reinforcement schedule before raising the criteria.

Either method works. The one you choose will probably depend on how methodical you are and how quickly you can raise the criteria.

If you are a dedicated keeper of records and are able to move forward in your training quickly, you'll probably do best with continuous reinforcement until reaching your final target behavior.

However, if you are less committed to keeping records and are less able to move ahead in your training, you might want to start introducing the variable reinforcement schedule earlier on. What we mean by being able to move ahead quickly in your training is that when you've reached one goal, you can easily move to the next. If you live in the city, work a full-time job, and are only able to go to the field on weekends, you will not be able to raise your criteria as quickly as the person who lives on 50 acres and doesn't work a traditional job.

To review reinforcement schedules, see Chapter 2.

Fading Reinforcers

Don't be in too much of a rush to fade your reinforcers. For some reason people tend to feel it is important for a dog to work purely for the joy of working. Hopefully, this will eventually happen; but first she has to learn the basics. In one sense, you fade your reinforcers every time you raise criteria, because you no longer reinforce for the lower criteria. However, you want to continue reinforcing until you are at your goal behavior.

Also keep in mind that once you're out in the field, the work itself will be reinforcing to your dog. Flushing, pointing, and retrieving are all intrinsically reinforcing behaviors. The trick is to be sure you've trained the basics properly before allowing your dog to be reinforced by these environmental reinforcers.

Once you reach your final goal behavior, you can begin fading the reinforcer. We recommend that you do this systematically, so you do not accidentally extinguish the behavior. We recommend starting with a 75% reinforcement ratio, then a 50% ratio, and, finally, a 25% ratio. You don't ever want to entirely stop reinforcing desired behavior; however, by the time you're at 25%, you'll probably be in the field and the work itself will be reinforcing for your dog.

To achieve a 75% ratio, reinforce all but the least satisfactory behaviors; for 50%, reinforce anything that is average or better; and for 25%, reinforce only the best behaviors. You should begin to see a general shift toward better performance, because that's what your dog is being reinforced for, so continue to shift your standard for what is a good performance, keeping the 80% rule in mind.

Basic Training

During all phases of training, log your dog's performance. (See Chapter 3 to review criteria setting and record keeping.) Do not move on to the next level until your dog is proficient at the current level. For most training, we recommend 80% proficiency; for recalls and remote sits, we recommend 100% proficiency.

Before you start training, invest in a three-ring binder and dividers. The binder will be your dog's training book; use the dividers to keep each behavior separate. Use sections at the back to store blank forms. We also recommend that you purchase a plastic zipper bag designed to fit in a three-ring binder; this bag will hold pens and pencils, extra clickers, and other useful small items.

Make it a habit to take your log book with you on your training expeditions. If you have a video camera, you might also want to take that. If you do, record yourself as often as you do your dog. You can also record your sessions on a small audio recorder and transcribe them into the log book later. Regardless of how you choose to record your sessions, do record them.

You will teach each behavior in three levels: basic, intermediate, and advanced. At the basic level you will train in a no-distraction environment and the goal will be to get the behavior and establish the cue. At the intermediate level you will begin generalizing the behavior and add minor distractions. Teach intermediate behaviors with the dog no further than 5–10 feet from you, with the exceptions of recalls and stays, which can be taught from up to 50–75 feet. At the advanced level, begin adding in distance and major distractions (these concepts are introduced at the end of this chapter; read them as soon as you're ready to progress to the advanced level).

In the intermediate and advanced sections of this chapter, we do not repeat the same instructions for each behavior that we describe in the basic section. However, if a behavior has training needs unique to that level, they are addressed.

Think about appropriate places to take your dog for training at intermediate and advanced levels. Some suggestions are busy parking lots (begin at the far end and work your way up to the stores), parks, parking lots where there will be dogs (vets, pet stores, groomers, and so on), and fields. Be careful about taking food into a dog park as it can create problems. However, if you know the dogs and it is not a busy time of day, you may be able to work with food.

We first discuss basic behaviors, then intermediate behaviors, and then advanced behaviors, in that order. When you start going to various locations to train intermediate and advanced behaviors, you will have the knowledge you need to train two or three behaviors in the same outing. When doing this, remember to give your dog a significant break—at least five to ten minutes—between sessions. You want to train only one behavior during any one training session.

Because some of the dog's behaviors that we want to reduce are intrinsically reinforcing (e.g., hunting or retrieving things other than what we want, peeing on bushes, and so on), we need reliable ways to interrupt the unwanted behavior so that we can set up another trial. Name recognition, attention commands, saying "whoa," and the whistle stop are particularly helpful. In addition, because we do not use punishment to reduce these behaviors, sometimes the order of training drills needs to be altered in order to ensure that the dog learns the proper behavior thoroughly before moving on.

If you are stuck or feeling frustrated, go back to Chapter 1 and review the basic learning principles. Something there should resonate.

Stages of Learning

Remember, there are four stages of learning: acquisition, fluency, generalization, and maintenance.

Acquisition

Acquisition is the stage in which the dog is learning the behavior and you are concerned with accurately teaching that behavior. There are different philosophies about training a new behavior. One school of thought is that you can train the behavior to a certain level and then later refine or add to the behavior to achieve the standard you actually want. Another school of thought is that you should train the behavior correctly from the beginning, as it is more difficult to change an existing behavior than it is to train a new behavior.

We are inclined to go with the second school of thought. We know (because it is one of the basic rules of learning) that a behavior that is reinforced is likely to be repeated. An example of training a behavior one way and then later changing it is when you first train for hunt tests and later train for field trials. In hunting, the requirement for the retrieve can sometimes be much less stringent than for tests or trials; for instance, in hunting the dog can drop the bird on the ground rather than delivering to hand as the dog must for tests and trials. If you originally train to meet casual hunting requirements, you will later have to *retrain* your dog to deliver the bird to hand. If you start by training the dog to deliver to hand, you won't have the problem of a previously reinforced, but now incorrect, behavior popping up at an inopportune moment.

As you learned in Chapter 3, there are ways to measure how well the dog has learned a behavior; by measuring compliance, you will be sure that the dog understands what she has been taught and be confident that you can raise your criteria.

Fluency

Fluency occurs when your dog is proficient at the behavior and doesn't have to think about it. A human analogy is driving a car. When you first learn to drive, you have to think about things like where the gas and brake pedals are, when and how to turn on the turn signals, and so on. After you've been driving for a while, these things are automatic and you don't have to think about them. Fluency comes with practice and repetition. However, you should not be working on fluency until your dog has acquired the behavior, or you run the risk of training unnecessary or undesired behaviors. Be sure your dog is performing the behavior correctly before starting on fluency.

Generalization

Generalization is probably one of the most neglected and misunderstood stages of learning. Generalizing is the ability to take acquired knowledge and apply it under different circumstances. A human analogy is learning trigonometry in a classroom and then going home and using it to design a tree house; a canine example is learning to heel in the backyard and then taking that to the field.

Humans are very good at generalizing. Dogs are only so-so; not nearly as good as we are. We tend to forget that they don't generalize as well as we do, and we assume that, because they know the behavior under a particular circumstance, they will be able to take that knowledge to other circumstances. You may need to actually retrain the behavior under various circumstances. This does not take long, because the dog does actually know the behavior, but don't expect her to go from place to place and perform the way she did where she was originally taught.

Maintenance

Maintenance is practicing a behavior the dog knows well. As with any skill, if you don't practice, you get rusty.

Maintenance continues throughout the dog's life.

Heel and Front Positions

Heel position is with your dog at your side, facing in the same direction as you. When heeling, your dog should automatically sit when you stop. Front position is with the dog facing you. Figure 4.1 shows the front and heel or "finish" position, as well as the two other core behaviors—sit-stay and walking to heel.

Basic Sit

Learning a basic sit is easy for most sporting dogs. It gets a little tougher when you get into the field and want them to sit while a bird is flying in front of their nose! The quickest way to teach a sit is to take a piece of food, put it in front of the dog's nose, and slowly move it over the top of the dog's head, making sure that the dog's nose is following the treat. Ideally, the dog's head will go up and her rump will go down—and there you have a sit!

4.1 The Basics

Sit and stay

Heel

Front

Finish

Occasionally, instead of the rump going down, the dog will back up. You can resolve this in two ways. One way is to place the dog with her back to a corner so she has nowhere to go, and then repeat the earlier exercise using the food lure. Another way is to stand in front of the dog with the treat and wait. As long as the dog is interested in the treat, she'll stay with you, and most dogs will eventually sit. As soon as her rump touches the floor, mark the behavior with either your clicker or a verbal marker such as "good!"

Once your dog will sit eight to ten times in a row with little or no hesitation and no intervening behaviors, add the cue. Be sure to say "sit" before your dog actually sits; remember, she knows what you want her to do, so for the cue to have meaning, it must happen before the behavior. When you've reached this point, stop reinforcing the sit unless you have cued it, as you don't want your dog sitting indiscriminately.

For the average gun dog, you should be able to get your dog to sit more than 45 times in 60 seconds. Run through this exercise before you move to the next level. Count out 60 treats, set your timer, and start working the sit. If your dog complies, you can confidently move to the intermediate level.

Using the techniques for criteria setting and record keeping established in Chapter 3, continue asking your dog to sit until you feel she really understands the cue.

Basic Heel

For gun dogs, "heel" is simply walking by your left side. It is not nearly as formal as a competition obedience heel. The dog's head and neck should be next to your leg and she should be within 1 to 2 feet from you. And, she should be able to do this off-leash! You can begin teaching this exercise in your house and yard off-leash; however, do begin adding the leash fairly soon, as you don't want your dog to learn to heel off-leash, but not on-leash.

Start by setting your criteria: distance, time, or number of steps you take. For example:

- **Distance** = every two feet you treat your dog for being in position

- **Time** = every two seconds you treat your dog for being in position

- **Steps** = every two steps you treat your dog for being in position

Once your dog is reliable at the current criteria, increase them a little bit. (Later in this chapter we cover more specific information on increasing criteria for adding in distance and duration.) Remember: if you have problems with the criteria you set, reduce them!

Once your dog is fairly reliable for 5 to 10 feet, add in the "heel" cue. Some people use their feet as a cue, that is, if you begin walking by moving your left leg, it is a cue to the dog to heel; if you begin walking by moving your right leg, it's a cue to the dog to stay.

Basic Stay

"Stay" is a behavior that few people train to reliability. However, if done properly, it is an easy behavior to train. Stay encompasses all the different components of a behavior—distance, duration, distraction, and handler orientation. Most owners concentrate only on distance and duration, which is why they end up with an unreliable behavior. Equally (if not more) important are owner orientation and distraction.

We'll begin with owner orientation, because that is the most difficult of the four components. Your first goal is to be able to walk around your dog. Once you can do that, you can begin adding in distance, duration, and distraction. We'll talk only briefly about duration, because you are automatically adding duration whenever you add distance.

We highly recommend that you practice your technique without the dog before you actually start training. The technique we teach here is similar to a choreographed dance; you need to practice or you will become confused about the order in which you perform certain behaviors.

Get a chair, and pretend that the chair is the dog until you have the routine fairly well worked out. Below is the routine, followed by specific details. Figure 4.2 diagrams the beginning steps of the routine, which should help you visualize the technique.

Initial stay routine

The initial stay training process has six steps:

1. Get into starting position, which is front position.
2. Give the dog the "stay" signal.
3. Bungee.
4. Return to starting position.
5. Treat the dog.
6. Repeat steps 1–5.

4.2 Sample Steps for Beginning Stay

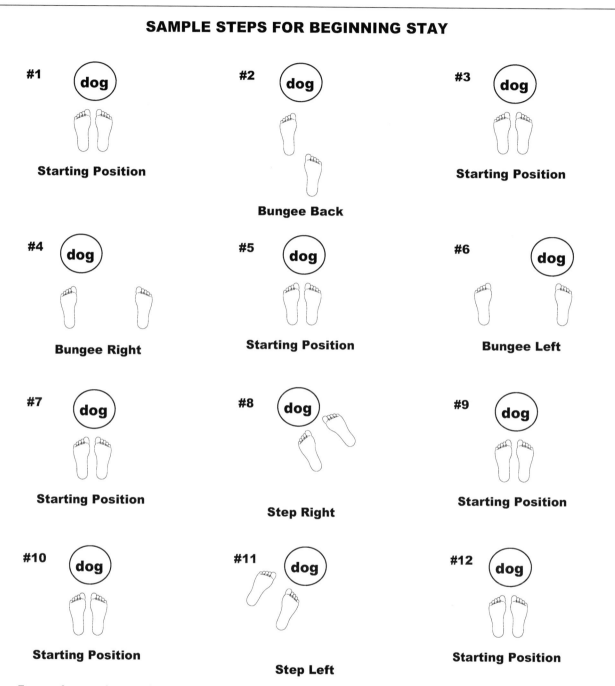

SAMPLE STEPS FOR BEGINNING STAY

#1 dog — Starting Position

#2 dog — Bungee Back

#3 dog — Starting Position

#4 dog — Bungee Right

#5 dog — Starting Position

#6 dog — Bungee Left

#7 dog — Starting Position

#8 dog — Step Right

#9 dog — Starting Position

#10 dog — Starting Position

#11 dog — Step Left

#12 dog — Starting Position

Except for starting position, repeat each position change until the dog is successful two times in a row. Remember—if the dog breaks twice in a row, you need to lower your criteria. Ideally, you will perform the criteria increase twice, the dog will be successful both times, and you will be able to increase your criteria with no unsuccessful trials. If this is not happening 80% of the time, you are increasing your criteria too much, and need to reassess.

Periodically, stop training and release your dog. You should be building on the previous stay, but you do not want to train too long or the dog will break—better that this is your decision!

Detailed instructions for the stay routine:

- Stay signal. Move the flat palm of your hand in toward the dog's face. DO NOT have the treat in the signal hand, or the dog may break the stay by following the treat.

- Bungee. Use one foot as a pivot foot; you do not move that foot initially. Once the dog is used to back, side, and forward movement, you can begin moving your pivot foot.

- Treat and repeat. Use these steps as an opportunity to build on your previous stay. When you treat the dog, just as the dog takes the treat from your hand, immediately reposition your hand so that it becomes the stay signal. Periodically release your dog. Don't leave her in a stay so long that she decides to break on her own.

- Setting criteria. This training goes quickly, if you do it properly. If you do a bungee and the dog is successful twice in a row, you can raise your criteria. If your dog is unsuccessful twice in a row, you need to lower your criteria. Ideally, you will be successful at least 80% of the time; the dog will not break at all, or rarely, if you are conscientious about your criteria jumps.

- Breaking the behavior down. If you cannot get your dog to stay at all, you need to really break the criteria down. It may be that you need to start by simply standing in front of your dog without moving for a count of one, then a count of two, and so on. Once you have a small bit of duration, you can start moving. Again, if you are having a hard time getting your dog to stay once you start moving, be aware of how much your body is moving. It may be that you need to keep your torso completely still and simply lift your leg from the knee down. We can always break behaviors down further—we just need to think about them and visualize what we're doing as if they were frames in a reel of film.

- Natural movement. It is common during the beginning stages of training a stay to move in slow motion. This can be very distracting to the dog. It is not a natural movement or a movement that they are familiar with. You will find that you have more success if you move naturally and at normal speed. If you are having a lot of problems with the stay, consider videotaping yourself. Watch how you are moving, as your movement is probably what is triggering your dog to break.

- Preparing to walk around the dog. This is probably the most difficult criterion the dog will encounter. Do not rush this step. Make sure everything you've done up to this point is solid. You should have been moving toward both the left and right sides of the dog. Once you are ready to take that jump and move around the dog, take a treat and hold it over the dog's nose (even touching, if necessary) as you circle behind her. This will keep her focused on the treat and less aware of you. Be careful not to step on her tail. Once you've gone around to the right, do it again without the treat on the nose. If you have problems, use the treat, but move it an inch or so away from her nose, and keep fading it until you can do away with the treat. Once you're successful circling from the right, you need to start over and circle from the left.

Basic Recall

Recalls are crucial to having a well-trained performance dog. As with any training, you begin with the fundamentals. Most of the training for recalls is described in the intermediate and advanced sections because it's easy to get your dog to respond to "come" in the house.

An easy way to get your dog to start paying attention to her name and to come when called is to do the "10-A-Day" exercise. Each morning, from the time you start until you feel she has a reliable recall, all members of the family should put 10 treats in their pocket and call the dog throughout the day, dispensing a treat each time the dog comes. Don't make her sit or do any other tasks—just reinforce her for coming when called.

Intermediate Sit

We will use the basic sit as the basis for all intermediate behaviors and will not repeat the instructions as we teach each new behavior.

Your dog must understand that the cue "sit" means to put her rump on the ground regardless of where she is in relation to you. You also want her to begin obeying commands under slightly distracting conditions.

Once your dog reliably sits on cue, it's time to start generalizing the behavior. Begin asking your dog to sit while she is in heel position. Once she reliably sits in heel position, start moving around; have your back to her or stand at an odd angle, sit on the couch and give the cue, lie on the floor and give the cue, stand on the couch and give the cue.

Don't be surprised if she walks over to you to sit. This is what she's been trained to do, and she has not yet learned to sit at a distance or at an odd angle to you. The easiest way to train this is to stand at a set distance from the dog, at any angle you choose, and measure for latency (see Chapter 3). After one set of latency trials, measure for compliance and adjust your criteria accordingly.

During intermediate training you'll also begin taking the behavior to different locations. Depending on where you normally begin training a new behavior, you'll gradually move your dog to more distracting environments. For instance, if you train the initial behavior in the living room, move to the kitchen, a bedroom, back deck, backyard, front porch, front yard, sidewalk, down the street, at the far end of the grocery store parking lot, and so on. You should pick a minimum of 10 diverse locations to train in. Remember that the more activity there is, the more distracting for the dog; also, the more dogs that frequent an area (whether they are present or not), the more distracting the environment.

Finally, you will introduce the whistle during intermediate training (detailed instructions are covered in Chapter 7). In general, putting the dog on whistle cue is the same as adding any new cue. (Adding a new cue is discussed later in this chapter.)

For most gun dogs, one blast on the whistle is the cue to sit.

Once your compliance and latency are at 80% at each of the locations you've trained in, you can begin the advanced level training.

Intermediate Heel

As with the sit, once you have a good, reliable behavior in familiar territory, it's time to start generalizing the behavior. Unlike the sit, you don't have to worry about handler orientation or heeling from a distance, since heel is about position. However, you do need to train the dog in different locations.

Intermediate Stay

In addition to generalizing the stay, you will also start adding distance when working on the intermediate stay. You've already installed the cue, so all you really have to do is begin practicing in different locations and gradually add in more distance. Each time you add distance, start by circling ¼ of the way around (that is, until you're facing the dog's side); then do a complete circle in both directions. Always be sure to circle around the dog before increasing distance.

You'll also begin generalizing your position—you may have your back or your side to her—and provide other distractions such as leaning over to pick things up. In a real field situation, you may do any number of things and will want your dog to maintain a stay, so this is the time to start practicing.

Begin having your dog stay while you do short, routine tasks such as making the bed, doing the dishes, taking out the garbage, and even mowing the lawn for short periods. Get her used to staying while you are doing other things and are not completely focused on her. This is where most dogs fall down; they do an excellent stay as long as the handler is focused on them, but as soon as the handler's attention is diverted, the dog breaks.

Intermediate Recall

Once your dog is reliably responding in the house, increase the difficulty slightly. Start taking the "10-A-Day" exercise out to the backyard, front yard, and other familiar locations. If you go to a dog park, start practicing there. If there are a lot of dogs at the park, you may want to substitute a game or toy for the treat. (Remember to be careful about bringing food into dog parks.)

Keep your dog within "critical distance." Critical distance is the point within which your dog obeys your commands and beyond which she doesn't. Depending on how long you've been training and under what types of circumstances, your dog will have a distance within which she will be reliable. That may be 5 feet, 10 feet, or 20 feet. It may also be only when she's on her leash. You can test her critical distance in places such as fenced dog parks. Let your dog get a few feet away and call her back. Do this several times; if she returns reliably, you're within her critical distance, and you can test her a few feet further out.

If you let your dog get beyond the critical distance, she will probably not return when you call her. Another thing to remember is that your dog's critical distance is different for each member of the family and in different locations. You always want to know and remember your dog's critical distance; if she's beyond that distance, don't try to get her back unless you're actively training for a further distance, or you'll weaken your cue.

Advanced Sit

We will use the basic sit as the basis for all advanced behaviors and will not repeat the instructions for sit as we teach each new behavior.

By the time you're at this level, your dog should be reliably sitting within 5 feet of you in every location and at every angle. Now it's time to start adding in distance and the distractions that make field training so challenging—and fun! For the sit, once you're

in the field you'll ultimately want reliability at 100 yards or more. Remember to start close, add a little distance, and then add in distraction. Once your dog is reliable under those circumstances, you can add more distance. See below for tips on adding in distance and distraction.

Advanced Heel

Now you can take it to the field! This is almost always your dog's most distracting environment, because she knows what's coming and will be very excited. Practice heeling a lot in the field. Work with other trainers to get your dog used to heeling around a lot of people and dogs: walk past birds in cages, walk past birds hidden in the brush, walk by birds sitting on the ground, and so on. Start with your dog on-leash, then graduate to off-leash. Remember to lower your criteria significantly and then build them back up. Reinforce liberally! Take your dog to trials, even if you are not competing, and work under those conditions.

Advanced Stay

Working the stay in the field is, again, your biggest challenge. You have less control over the environment and less control over your dog. Be sure to set the stage for success: start close to your dog then work your way out—don't move forward too quickly—and make certain your dog is steady before raising your criteria.

Advanced Recalls

Once your dog is reliable within her critical distance, you can start adding more distractions. It's important to do distraction training before adding too much distance. An important principle of training is to control the environment; the further away your dog is, the less control you have over the environment. If you train your dog to respond to distractions before she gets too far from you, it will be easier to add distance and maintain reliability.

When training for distractions, it's essential to start by having control over your dog. Reduce the critical distance by at least half, maybe more. If you don't have a fenced area to work in, use your long line as a safety; if your dog takes off and you can't get her back, she is learning that she doesn't have to listen to you. Never call your dog if you know she isn't going to come. Here are rules for training both distraction and distance:

- If the dog does not respond to the command twice in a row, cut your distance in half, and then add in more distance slowly.

- If the dog responds to the command five times in a row, you can increase your distraction slightly.

If you are setting good criteria increases, you shouldn't have to decrease distance more than once every five to ten criteria increases. If you find you are having to back up a lot, rethink your criteria jumps—they're probably too much for the dog.

Once you feel your dog is 100% reliable in a highly distracting environment within her critical distance, you can start adding distance. During this phase be even more cautious than usual. Don't get cocky: remember that every time your dog doesn't respond to your cue, she's being reinforced by the environment and learning to disregard the recall cue.

They Love to Run!

One of the most frequent concerns among members of our e-mail discussion lists is that their gun dogs run away and get so involved in hunting up critters that they won't come back when called. Here are some things you can do about your running dog.

First, build a strong bond with your dog from the beginning. Practice benign leadership by controlling all of the resources that your dog desires: food, treats, toys, games, walks, petting, praise, and so on. Implement a Nothing in Life is Free (NILIF) program by having your dog do some simple obedience task to earn all of his privileges.

Second, don't let the dog get into the habit of running free. Even if you have a large, safe yard, keep your dog close on a leash when he is a puppy. Start with a short leash, and graduate to a longer leash or check cord (see Chapter 5). Get your dog used to being around you and he will be less likely to initiate runaways.

Third, reward your dog enthusiastically for staying near and paying attention. Click and treat for eye contact and for staying in close range. Keep your dog's attention focused on you and try to be more interesting than the dirt that he wants to sniff!

Fourth, follow the instructions in this chapter for training a recall. Don't let your dog run off-leash until you are confident that you can get him back. And, even then, punctuate his off-leash sessions with recall and other obedience tasks. Help him to learn that being close, and following your cues, is highly rewarding.

Finally, work on an emergency recall. We like the method developed by Leslie Nelson, a sight hound trainer from Connecticut. She uses high-value rewards (what she calls "fine dining") to classically condition an emergency word that is different from the regular recall. By practicing this "really reliable recall" several times each day, she ensures that it will be available when it is really needed. You can find out more by ordering her DVDs from Tawzer Dog Videos.

Adding A New Cue

To add a new cue:

1. Give the new cue.
2. Follow with the established cue.
3. Repeat five to ten times.
4. Give the new cue without following up with the established cue.
5. If the dog responds, continue giving the new cue until it is well established.
6. If the dog does not respond, repeat steps 1–4.

Be sure to give the new cue *first*; if you give the two cues at the same time, you'll block the new cue (see Chapter 1).

Overshadowing and Blocking

Overshadowing occurs when you give two conditioned stimuli (cues) at the same time and, because one is more obvious, the dog associates only the more obvious stimulus with the unconditioned stimulus. Remember, a conditioned stimulus is a stimulus that has been associated with an unconditioned stimulus. Blocking happens when you attempt to condition a new stimulus, but the new stimulus gives the dog no new information because it is blocked by the original conditioned stimulus. Overshadowing and blocking are classical (Pavlovian or respondent) learning.

However, they also relate to operant learning and affect how well an animal learns to distinguish cues. Take these three criteria into consideration when training a cue:

- **Novelty.** It has been shown that the more novel the cue, the more quickly the animal will associate that cue with the behavior. So be sure to pick a cue that you have not used for any other behavior.

- **History.** The stronger the history of the cue, the more likely the animal will ignore other stimuli and respond to the cue. Train, train, train—under achievable conditions—and gradually increase difficulty.

- **Salience.** The easier the cue is to distinguish from other stimuli, the more likely the animal will respond appropriately. The dog will notice and understand large, gross movements more easily than subtle movements.

Especially in field training, these concepts are huge! There are so many strong stimuli in the field that it is very easy for the dog to get sidetracked. If you keep these three criteria in mind when training, you'll have more success getting your dog under stimulus control.

Keep-Going Signals or Intermediate Bridge

A keep-going signal (KGS) or intermediate bridge (IB) is a signal to the dog that he is carrying out a behavior that will ultimately result in delivery of a primary reinforcer. Trainers have used these signals with marine mammals and birds engaged in long distance work. You can think of the KGS/IB in two ways:

1. As a conditioned tertiary reinforcer. The KGS/IB predicts the secondary reinforcer (click), which predicts the primary reinforcer (treat or other reinforcer).
2. As a cue to continue the current behavior.

These ways of thinking are not mutually exclusive. In fact, you can think of any cue as a tertiary reinforcer in the sense that the behavior it signals has a reinforcement history (assuming you're using a secondary reinforcer).

Used in this scenario, you condition the KGS/IB by pairing it first with a conditioned secondary reinforcer, followed by a primary reinforcer. For example, the trainer might say "keep going" followed by C/T. For a discrete behavior, such as picking up a dummy correctly, a discrete marker such as the single phrase "keep going" is appropriate. For a continuous behavior, such as running along a straight line, it's more effective to use a continuous signal, such as the "praise tone" on some electronic collars. This signifies to the dog that, as long as he hears the tone, he is on the right track.

It is useful to begin conditioning the discrete KGS relatively early in the training process; however, a continuous tone signals a concept rather than a specific behavior and is best postponed until after the dog has mastered a range of complex behaviors, including long behavior chains and modifier cues such as direction.

Another approach is to use the secondary reinforcer (click) at stages along the retrieving behavior chain to signal successful completion of the intermediate activity. Because much of gun dog work, including continuing to hunt or retrieve, is intrinsically reinforcing, the click should maintain its power, even if there is a delay in delivering a primary reinforcer at the end of the chain. This is also true for other behavior chains such as quartering, hunting, pointing, and flushing.

Distance and Duration

With both distance and duration, once you have some reliability, start mixing up the criteria. By this we mean that most of the time the criterion is what you're working on, but vary it so that sometimes you do more and sometimes less. For instance, if you are working on a distance of 20 feet, perform most of your trials at 20 feet, but some at 10 feet, some at 15, and some at 25. This will keep your dog from predicting what she's supposed to do and will keep the reinforcer more interesting!

Distance

Add in distance 1 to 3 feet at a time. Once your dog is reliable at 15 feet, you can start adding distance in 5-foot increments; once she's reliable at 30 feet, you can start increasing in 10-foot increments. As she gets reliable further out, you can use your judgment about how much distance to add, but if at any time she does not comply twice in a row or two out of five times, you need to back up to a point at which she is very reliable and start over.

The best way to add distance is to start in your original no-distraction area, add in as much distance as you can in that location, then move to

the next location (such as the kitchen or bedroom), add in as much distance as you can, and keep progressing to new locations.

Distractions

You start adding in distraction the same way you do distance: start in your no-distraction area and move to the next location when your dog reaches 80% compliance. You can add in your distance in the no-distraction area, add in distractions, move to the next low-distraction area, add in your distance, then the distraction, and so on. Or you can add in all of your distance, then all of your distraction. It doesn't matter, as long as you do it in a methodical manner and your dog has reached 80% compliance at every level prior to moving on.

When you add a new distraction, cut the distance to at least half—more if necessary. Again, it sounds like a lot of work, but it goes quickly and it takes a lot less time and frustration than going back and retraining when you find out your dog isn't really trained to the level you thought.

Here is a list of possible distractions you can do around the house, yard, and other familiar locations.

- You running, skipping, and jumping
- Another familiar adult in the room
- Another familiar adult running, skipping, and jumping
- Familiar child in the room
- Familiar child running, skipping, and jumping
- Two to three people milling about, including children
- A party
- Another dog on-leash
- Another dog off-leash
- Several dogs (a party!)
- Rolling a tennis ball past your dog
- Tossing a tennis ball
- Tossing a happy bumper
- Familiar cat (assuming your dog is cat friendly)
- Tossing a frozen bird
- Tossing a thawed bird
- A live bird

Once you get to the field, start proofing for the unique distractions you will find there. Some examples are the following:

- Gunshots (make sure your dog has been desensitized to guns first)
- Other hunters with dogs on-leash
- Other hunters with dogs off-leash
- You kicking at the brush (to simulate noise the dog might hear in the field)
- Object hidden in brush and tied to a long string (which allows you to make noises without being close to the noise or the dog)
- Other dogs hunting

Add to this list as you see fit. Think of everything you might run into in the field and proof your dog for it *before* she's exposed under working conditions.

If you do your proofing properly, you'll have a much steadier dog. Proofing is an area in which it's worthwhile to take your time and do it right. Most trainers who jump ahead too quickly end up backing up a little, retraining, then finding out that the dog still isn't thoroughly trained, so they go back a little further. This takes much more time than training properly. Get into the frame of mind in which you enjoy the moment and aren't obsessed with the end goal. After all, that's what it's really all about!

Leave It

Among the essential skills for a gun dog are leaving something alone when asked or giving an object (like a bird) up on command. Here are some ways to train this behavior, based on a method used by Carole Peeler, a Certified Pet Dog Trainer (CPDT) in Falls Church, Virginia.

- Start by teaching your dog to back away from something that you control. To do so, first put some small treats in your fist and say "leave it." Watch your dog patiently and when she moves away from your fist, say "take it," and pop a treat up for her to take. (This may take a while—be patient!) Depending on the dog, you may have to catch an instant when the dog removes her nose

from your hand; some dogs are more persistent that others! Also be prepared for the dog to paw or bite at your hand. Practice many times until the dog backs away instantly when you say "leave it."

- To add duration to leave it/take it, start again with treats in your fist. Then, say "leave it." Silently count to three. If the dog stays and leaves it, say "take it," and give the treat. If not, say "leave it" again (in a calm tone of voice) and wait until the dog learns to stay away for a count of three. Do this several times and then vary the count (three, one, five, two, one, three, and so on). Build up to five to seven seconds. If necessary, reduce the amount of time you require the dog to leave it and build up to a count of three.

- Keep working on leave it/take it and gradually move the treat out of your hand and onto your knee, then foot, then the floor. Keep moving the treat until it is just over halfway between you and the dog, putting the treat in the dog's "possession zone."

- If the dog backs away from treats in his possession zone, keep moving until you can place it very close to, or touching, the dog. If not, or if the dog has guarding issues, do not proceed until you have desensitized the dog to removal of a valued object.

- Once the dog is comfortable leaving a treat that you have placed nearby, try a "toy trade" with an object of low to moderate value. Gradually increase the value of objects traded. When you prepare your dog for field work, you will train him to drop a dummy, a frozen bird, a thawed bird, a freshly killed bird, and eventually a live bird.

Once you have covered basic obedience with your gun dog, you can move on to more specialized training. We'll start with retrieving—a skill common to almost all gun dogs—and then describe how to train other gun dog tasks. But first we'll review some of the additional steps you should take to get you and your dog ready for the field.

Chapter 5
Into the Field

He Can Sit ... Now What?

Once you and your dog have mastered some key obedience skills, you will be eager to get out and work. In this chapter we'll cover some of the topics that you will need to consider before heading out to the field with your dog. These topics include: information about gun dog breeds, their characteristics, and their work; equipment you will need to train effectively; and safety and health considerations. We'll also discuss selection of training locations and some of the places where you and your dog can get support for your training efforts.

Gun Dogs: What They Are and What They Do

The first thing you will need in order to begin training is a dog! The American Kennel Club includes gun dogs in the Sporting Group. There are currently 26 breeds listed in this group:

- American water spaniel
- Brittany
- Chesapeake Bay retriever
- Clumber spaniel
- Cocker spaniel
- Curly-coated retriever
- English cocker spaniel
- English setter
- English springer spaniel
- Field spaniel
- Flat-coated retriever
- German shorthaired pointer
- German wirehaired pointer
- Golden retriever
- Gordon setter
- Irish setter
- Irish water spaniel
- Labrador retriever
- Nova Scotia duck tolling retriever

- Pointer
- Spinone Italiano
- Sussex spaniel
- Vizsla
- Weimaraner
- Welsh springer spaniel
- Wirehaired pointing griffon

Gun dogs fall into roughly three subgroups, depending on their particular tasks in the field. Flushing dogs like spaniels search for birds within gunshot range from the hunter. When they locate a bird, they flush it into the air and then retrieve the bird when it is shot. Pointing breeds, including those with "pointer" in their name as well as setters and several others, hunt and point game. In the United States, the practice is that the game is flushed by the hunter; in other countries the dogs may flush on command. Pointers must then retrieve on both land and water.

5.1 Bentley

An eight-month-old English setter with a Beginner Retriever title.

45

Retrievers, of course, retrieve! They are used mainly in hunting waterfowl and must bring back birds from long distances, over land and water, in icy conditions, and in difficult terrain. Many retrievers also are good upland hunters.

5.2 Friskie

Yellow Labrador from field lines.

Some gun dogs are "versatile hunting breeds," defined by the North American Versatile Hunting Dog Association (NAVHDA) on its website (www. navhda.org/breeds.html) as "the dog that is bred and trained to dependably hunt and track game, to retrieve on both land and water, and to track wounded game on both land and water." They include the pointing breeds and the Weimaraner, vizsla, Brittany, and spinone. The three setter breeds—Gordon, English, and Irish—are also quite versatile, although they are not included in the NAVHDA registry.

And there are other breeds, not part of the Sporting Group, that can perform well in the field, including poodles and Portuguese water dogs.

The exact behaviors you will train, and the sequence in which you will train them, will depend on the breed and the purpose of your training. The exercises at various levels in hunt tests and field trials are clearly established (see Appendix II), so if competi-

tion is your goal, structure your program along the lines of the progression of tests or trials. On the other hand, if your objective is a reliable hunting companion, craft your training to suit the kind of hunting you plan to do.

5.3 Port

A standard poodle with his first shot flyer! (Photo by Tara Yates. Used with permission.)

Gun Dog Care

We will not cover general dog care in this book, as there are many fine books on dog and puppy health, nutrition, and socialization. We do want to point out, however, several common characteristics of gun dogs that will affect how you care for them.

Gun dogs are bred to work closely with their people. They thrive on attention and companionship. This poses a challenge for owners who want their family dogs to do double-duty as gun dogs. In parts of the United States and United Kingdom, gun dog owners relegate their dogs to an outdoor kennel, to be brought out only to train or hunt. For some dogs, their routine includes only training, walking to heel, and hunting, with little time for companionship or play. The rationale is that this facilitates training, especially at the higher levels. In this book, however, we focus on dogs that have regular access to the home and family and engage in activities other than hunting. We acknowledge that this can complicate training, but we see gun dogs as family dogs as much as hunting dogs. There is nothing more heartwarming than a black Lab (or a springer or a Brittany) curled up on a rug by the fireplace while the family watches TV. And the dogs seem to agree!

Gun dogs are high-energy canines. In some breeds (Labs, for instance), there is a division between dogs bred for show and those bred for field work, with the latter being even higher in energy. So gun dogs require much more than the average half-hour a day of aerobic exercise that all healthy adult dogs need. For an active German shorthair, quartering fields for six hours with a dozen retrieves is just a warm-up! So if you don't hunt frequently, find another outlet for your dog's energy such as jogging, swimming, hiking, or an organized dog sport such as agility or flyball. Three strolls around the neighborhood each day just won't cut it!

Good nutrition is a need related to exercise. In the world of dog foods, there are roughly three categories: supermarket-grade kibble (the canine equivalent of junk food), "premium" dog foods (adequate but nothing special), and high-quality organic or natural foods that provide superior nutrition. Another recent development in canine nutrition is the availability of freeze-dried, raw-food diets that are said to simulate a dog's natural diet. Whatever you choose to feed your gun dog, we recommend that you do your research, read labels carefully, and choose a high-quality food that suits your dog's active lifestyle.

As active, outdoor animals, gun dogs need sound health. Check with your vet about required and recommended vaccinations. Many hunting areas are infested with rabid raccoons, skunks, and other nasty critters. We strongly recommend that you use a periodic flea and tick preventative and discuss Lyme disease inoculations with your vet. Lyme disease is a terrible disease for both dogs and humans, and is endemic in many hunting areas. Be sure to schedule regular checkups and monitor the dog's

general health carefully. It's important to keep your dog's ears clean, especially after swimming. And check the paws and pads for cuts and abrasions, and treat them promptly to avoid infections.

Finally, know that gun dogs are smart! Of course all of your dogs have been smart. But these breeds have a particular need to be mentally active. Gun dogs are not couch potatoes; nor are they lazy students. They want to learn new things, not just practice the things they already know. So it's always a good idea to have some new training tasks on the agenda. Fortunately there's always a new skill that a gun dog can learn, a more interesting location to train, or a new prey to pursue. And, when you're not training, be sure to provide stimulating, interactive toys and chew objects to keep your dog occupied.

Equipment

Whichever breed you choose, there is some basic equipment that you will need.

Of course, as a positive trainer you will need a clicker (or verbal reward marker) as well as treats, tug toys, and other reinforcers for your dog. You will also need some good chew toys, bones, and so forth to serve as reinforcers after a training session, or to keep your dog occupied while waiting for a turn to train. And you will need a good supply of water; a collapsible canvas bowl can be very useful.

You'll also need the flat buckle or snap collar and 6-foot leash that you used for your dog's basic obedience training. In addition, for field work, it's a good idea to get a "check cord" to help control your dog. This is a long lead, usually 30 to 50 feet in length, that clips onto the collar. Depending on your training objective and the dog's level of proficiency, you can either hold on to the line, or you can let your dog drag it if you are confident that you can always get within 30 to 50 feet.

5.4 Check Cord

The check cords made from polypropylene resist snagging and also float.

It's also useful to have a "slip cord" that you can use to control your dog on the retrieving line. This is a braided cord that you can attach to your belt and slip through the ring on your dog's collar. When you send the dog to retrieve, you simply let go of the cord and it slips free of the collar.

5.5 Slip Cord

Useful for steadying a young dog. They can be used in early US tests, but not British!

Another point to keep in mind: check and slip cords can give you nasty burns when the dog is taking off. Get some good work gloves and always use them when you are handling your dog on a line.

If you have a pointing or flushing dog, you need a way to locate her in the field and to know when she is on point. The traditional method is to put a bell on the dog's collar. When she is moving you will hear it; when she stops, the sound stops. There are also "tracking collars" (not to be confused with shock or electronic collars) that emit different noises when a dog is moving and when she is on point. And there are even collars with global positioning system (GPS) transmitters so you can track your dog when she's out ahead of you! There are collars under development that have a clicker or another sound so that you can give a "reward marker" to your dog at a distance. Many positive trainers think that, at the moment, these are not particularly helpful because there is a time delay before the signal is activated. But eventually these tools might be useful with dogs that benefit from the feedback that they are progressing in the right direction.

You will also need a whistle to signal your dog. There are several varieties available, and online gun dog supply houses have many types. Some come with a "pea" that provides a trill, while others are "pea-less." You can also get whistles with a cone-like covering (see Figure 5.6) that direct the sound outward, making it easier for your dog to hear and saving your eardrums from that high-pitched sound. Use a lanyard to hold your whistle and clicker, but be warned: when you take your dog to a training session you will probably be the only person there with a clicker on your lanyard. Be prepared to explain what it is and also to take a little heat for using "soft" methods to train a gun dog.

Another item to put on your lanyard is a bird call. They come in many varieties and price ranges. There are calls for ducks, quail, pheasant, hawks, turkeys, and other birds. A serious duck hunter can spend $100 or more for a call, but for basic training you can get by with an inexpensive call such as the ones pictured in Figure 5.6.

5.6 Lanyards and Whistles

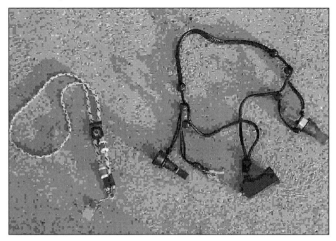

Left: Lanyard with clear whistle, compass, and flush counter for upland hunting. Right: Lanyard with "mega-whistle" and duck calls for waterfowling.

For the retrieving part of your training, you will need training dummies. These are sometimes called "bumpers" because some types were initially used by boaters, placed between the hull and pier to prevent damage from bumping. (We use the terms "dummy" and "bumper" interchangeably in this book.) Training dummies come in several sizes, colors, and types. Pick a size that fits your dog's mouth comfortably for initial training, and gradually increase the size over time. We usually begin our training with a 1½-inch knobby, rubber dummy, then progress to a 3-inch canvas dummy. For ease of visibility for the dog, white or black-and-white dummies work best in the yard or field. Orange dummies are more difficult for the dog to see against a green or brown background and are best reserved for more advanced training. (You can also get orange poles or tape to mark locations where you plant dummies or birds, so that you know where they are, but the dog doesn't. These are helpful for "blind retrieves" as described in Chapter 7.) If you want to make the dummies more exciting for your dog, and easier to locate, you can purchase bird scent and spread it on or inject it into the dummies.

5.7 Training Dummies

From left to right: 1½-inch orange, 1½-inch white, 3-inch canvas, Dead Fowl Trainer duck, Dead Fowl Trainer pheasant.

An alternative (or a complement) to the training dummy is a Dead Fowl Trainer, sometimes called a Dokken, after its inventor. This is a molded rubber dummy in the shape of a bird, with a hinged head to simulate the weight and feel of a real fowl (see Figure 5.7). They come in a variety of species—ducks, geese, and pheasant—and colors. A puppy trainer comes in the size and color of a blue-winged teal. Some Dokkens can be fitted with wings and there is a "diving" version that attaches to a fishing line to mimic the movement of a duck in the water. You can inject Dead Fowl Trainers with bird scent. They are very useful for improving a dog's hold on an actual bird.

Two other devices, though fairly expensive, can add a lot to your (and your dog's) training enjoyment.

One of these devices is a handheld dummy launcher (see Figure 5.8). Handheld launchers are available in a couple of brands, both of which function in the same way: you load a dummy with a hollow metal tube in the center onto a launching device that propels the dummy with a .22 caliber blank charge. (The charges come in various sizes, and can throw a dummy from about 40 to more than 70 yards.) Many dogs love to retrieve dummies from these launchers, as the launchers generate a lot of noise and motion. They are also useful for helping dogs get used to gunshots, doing water retrieves at distances longer than you can throw, and setting up blind retrieves across water.

5.8 Handheld Launcher

The shoulder stock will save on skinned knuckles.

The other device is a remote launcher (see Figure 5.9). There are many types, ranging from simple catapults to multiple bumper launchers, and they vary in price from a few hundred to more than a thousand dollars. These devices operate from an electronic remote control to release a dummy, Dead Fowl Trainer, or bird on command. Many also have speakers that make bird noises and slots for blank cartridges that fire when the launcher is triggered. These are invaluable for the handler who has to train alone yet needs to extend the distance of a retrieve and provide realistic conditions for the dog.

5.9 Remote Launcher

This lightweight launcher can throw a bird 25 yards and be set off more than 100 yards from the handler.

For conditioning your dog to tolerate gunfire, it's helpful to have some guns! A good way to begin is with a starter's pistol that can fire .22 blanks. At some point, you will want to transition to shotgun fire and use blank "poppers" to help your dog become used to the shot. Because you will be carrying a gun into the field, or in a hunt test, you may want to get a wooden "handler's gun" that you can use to help your dog acclimate to an object being in your hand. (See Figure 5.10.)

5.10 Gun Conditioning Equipment

Shotgun, handler's gun, and starter's pistol—and don't forget the ear protectors!

We recommend some other training and safety equipment. Be sure that you have a good first-aid kit and have a good book on treatment of common injuries at hand. Carry a knife, sunscreen, and insect repellent. During hunting season, be sure to dress appropriately, including blaze-orange clothing when in upland bird hunting areas. For waterfowl areas, camouflage clothing and a good pair of waders (or at least high boots) are the norm. And you may want to consider a vest for your dog—either a blaze-orange vest for protection or a flotation vest for rough water. Dog boots can also protect dogs' feet in rough terrain.

The most important piece of equipment, of course, is birds! Depending on the stage of training, you may want live or dead birds, small birds such as quail, or full-grown ducks. You can usually obtain birds from game farms or large poultry-supply companies. You can find good Internet listings for both. Be sure to check your local regulations regarding import and use of birds and disposal of bird carcasses.

Equipment That You Won't Need

Choke and pinch collars (sometimes called "training" and "prong" collars) are aversive devices that use "positive punishment" to change dogs' behavior. They cause discomfort on the neck and windpipe when the handler jerks on the leash to give a "correction." We don't use them. We believe that the use of aversives is not necessary or efficient in teaching dogs what we want them to do. Punishment, by definition, can only decrease the probability of an unwanted behavior; it cannot teach the desired behavior. We prefer to elicit the preferred behavior and then reinforce its repetition, rather than waiting for the dog to make a mistake and then correcting it. This strikes us as both more effective and more humane.

Also, unlike most American gun dog trainers, we do not use shock or electronic collars. These are devices that fit around the dog's neck and contain small electrodes that contact the dog's skin and, when activated, send a burst of electricity between the contacts through the dog's neck to punish the dog for unwanted behavior. Modern shock collars have a variety of settings for intensity and length of the shock, and can be triggered at great distances.

Mike Lardy, a prominent trainer, described a dog's first reactions to shock collars in this way: "Dogs have a variety of reactions to the first burn (shock). One may holler and jump, another may simply drop his ears and lower his head" ("Collar Conditioning," *The Retriever Journal*, June/July 1996, p. 41). A study by Matthijs B.H. Schilder and Joanne A.M. van der Borg, "Training Dogs With the Help of the Shock Collar: Short and Long Term Behavioural Effects" (*Applied Animal Behaviour Science* 85, 2004, pp. 319–334), reported significantly increased signs of stress among dogs that had been shocked—lower ear and tail positions, high-pitched yelps, squealing, avoidance behavior, and occasional aggression.

These descriptions confirm that shock collars, like choke and pinch collars, are fundamentally aversive. They function by using positive punishment or negative reinforcement—shocking a dog until it complies with the desired command. We choose not to use these techniques except when the dog's life may be at stake, as in snake aversion training. We acknowledge that almost all of the high-performing field trial dogs, and many fine hunting companions, have been trained using these devices. However, we also note that in other dog sports—including agility, competitive obedience, and even protection work—the use of aversives is on the decline. Our hope is that by using some of the methods outlined in this book, trainers will begin to work with gun dogs without using shock collars, and thus positive training methods will gradually infiltrate this field as well.

A related note: Electric or "invisible" fences use essentially the same technology as shock collars. We recommend that you use other means to contain your dog and do not subject a good gun dog to electric shocks. Besides having a potentially negative impact on your dog, electric shocks for containment can disturb your training as well.

Where to Train?

Most gun dog training programs make a distinction between "yard" and "field" training. The yard is a low distraction area, with little vegetation cover and few (ideally no) animals for your dog to scent or chase. This is where you first try out your new training concepts. Only when she has been thoroughly proofed in the yard do you take the dog to a more distracting location and try to generalize the response. We think it can be useful to have a couple of intermediate steps before you actually go into a hunting area. One is another "yard," perhaps a ball field or fenced area in a park where you can expose your dog to a few more distractions while still focusing on skill building. Another is a "training field," an area where there is more varied terrain and cover, and where birds and other animals may be present, but not as filled with game as a real hunting preserve or wildlife management area. Many hunt tests are held in such areas. Only after proofing commands in those locations would we recommend taking your dog into an area with abundant game.

Your training location also requires access to water. The ideal pond for initial training will have a gradual slope to the water, low vegetation, and a few points of land where you can station a bird-thrower or a remote launcher. As training progresses, you can add more challenging water locations such as tidal marshes, seacoast beaches, and lakes with heavy undergrowth. Be sure to check the tide tables for your area and to inspect carefully for rocks, tree branches, and other obstacles. For early training, you will want to ensure that the dog does not have an unpleasant initial experience in the water, so avoid water work until the water temperature reaches 50 degrees or so. A further caution: if you are training in a park or wildlife management area where fishing is allowed, be sure to check carefully on land and in the water for fishhooks and other debris that can injure your dog or make her ill.

Training Resources

You are in good company in training your gun dog. There are lots of other people out there who are happy to help. A good place to start is with breed clubs. Most regional gun dog breed organizations have field training and test programs. Many have access to good field locations and birds as well. Check your national breed club's website for the locations of regional clubs near you. National gun dog clubs welcome a variety of breeds. Examples are the American Hunting Dog Club (www.ahdc.org) and the Hunting Retriever Club (www.hrc-ukc.com), which is affiliated with the United Kennel Club (UKC).

Another potential source for training assistance is your state's Department of Environmental Management or equivalent organization. This office will know the state-managed hunting areas and also the private hunt clubs and preserves. Many of the staff members are hunters or gun dog owners. You may even be able to find a training partner there.

There are several good sources of gun dog training information on the Internet. They include the North

American Hunting Retriever Association (NAHRA) and NAVHDA websites, Working Retrieval Central, and two periodicals, *The Retriever Journal* (www.retrieverjournal.com) and *The Pointing Dog Journal* (www.pointingdogjournal.com). We've listed a number of sites, along with books and videos, in Appendix I, but we want to mention two Internet forums in particular here. The first is the PositiveGunDogs Yahoo Group discussion list. The list now has more than 300 members, all of whom are interested in positive training methods for hunting, tests, and trials. Some are very experienced; others are novices. But all are very supportive and willing to answer questions for "newbies," or new members. To join, go to http://groups.yahoo.com and follow the instructions to set up a personal account. Then subscribe to the PositiveGunDogs Yahoo Group by sending an e-mail to PositiveGunDogs-subscribe@yahoogroups.com.

Another excellent resource is the Gundog and Bird Dog Forums, managed by British trainer Eric Begbie. (We have drawn on Begbie's excellent program for many of the ideas in this book.) There are individual discussion groups for training gun dogs, tests and trials, health, and breeding. To join, go to www.less-stress.com/discuss2 and follow the instructions.

The Way Ahead

Now that you have a dog, all of your stuff, a place to train, and lots of support, it's time to really get into gun dog training. Move on to the next chapter, and have fun!

They All Have to Do It!

Unless you use your dog purely for pointing, your gun dog will at some point have to retrieve game. And, if you are not a hunter but just want to have fun in the field with your dog, retrieving is a joyful and exciting activity. So in this chapter, we provide a systematic method for teaching your dog to retrieve on command.

Puppy Play

As soon as your puppy comes home, you can begin to play retrieving games and check out her retrieve instinct. Begin by tossing a soft, light object in the hall, so she can't run away with it. Don't give any commands; just see if she chases after the toy. Most puppies from good hunting stock will do it by nature. But they are puppies—everything is interesting and distractions abound—so keep it light and fun. If she doesn't come back readily, you can coax her back with a treat. You can also have a second toy that you toss in the opposite direction, so she has to run by you to get it. She'll probably drop the first one to get the second, but even if she doesn't, she'll be learning that returning to you gets her a great reinforcer—something else to chase!

Keep up the fetching game while you work on your basic obedience. You can focus especially on some of the basic behaviors that will be important when your pup is becoming a skilled retriever, such as sit, stay, walking at heel, going out from your side, and dropping objects on command. Don't push the retrieving; two or three short fetches at a time are plenty for a young pup.

Many retriever trainers recommend that you wait until your puppy is about six months old and has her permanent teeth before you teach her to retrieve in response to a command. In the old days, this was because most trainers used choke collars as part of the training process and assumed that dogs had to be this age before they could tolerate this method. But there is also a real concern that younger puppies that are teething may be uncomfortable or they may chew to relieve the discomfort, leading the owners to get frustrated and impatient with the puppies. This is why it is essential that you know your dog. We have seen dogs learn to retrieve on command earlier than six months, but monitor your pup carefully and take a break if she shows signs of oral discomfort.

Another good reason to wait before training the retrieve is to ensure that your basic obedience is highly reliable. In particular, you need to have the tools to handle or interrupt your dog's behavior at a distance. Therefore, we strongly recommend concentrating on basic skills, especially the whistle stop (see Chapter 7) and the recall (see Chapter 4) before venturing too far into the field.

You Have to Teach Them to Retrieve?

Yes, you do! Even if your puppy has the greatest retrieving instinct in the canine world, she still needs to learn some key skills. These include fetching the proper objects (the bird, not the dead fish), in the proper order (the cripple first, so it doesn't escape), at long distances, and over difficult terrain or in icy water. Another key skill for retrievers is not retrieving until commanded to do so by remaining steady in the blind, boat, or at the line in a trial. This skill is also important so the dog doesn't interfere with the hunt and possibly get injured in the process. Flushers need to learn to sit immediately after the flush, yet they are allowed to grab a bird in flight, so this is a fairly complex behavior involving both impulse control and judgment! Retrieving is a complex and challenging behavior to teach and requires patience, consistency, and a step-by-step approach.

You also have to teach your dog to retrieve things she hasn't seen fall. In the field, there's no guarantee that your dog will be looking directly at the bird as it falls, so she has to be able to run out on your command and search for it, taking direction from you as necessary. In this chapter, we will discuss how to train your dog to find game it has seen fall. This is called a "marked" retrieve. In the next chapter, we will deal with "blind" retrieves, in which the dog is directed by the handler to the right area, where it hunts and completes the retrieve.

Yard and Field Work

When you are teaching a skill as complex as retrieving, it's important to begin with the basics and to work in a quiet area. So you will begin your training in the "yard." Yard work is the training that you do in your living room, backyard, or in another place with very few distractions. Only when you and your dog have mastered a skill in the yard will you take it into the "field." The field is a place where there are live birds, varying terrain and vegetation, other dogs, people, guns, vehicles, and other things that distract your dog and may cause her anxiety. In Chapter 1, when we discussed the principles of learning, we said that they included acquisition, fluency, generalization, and maintenance. A fundamental principle of retriever training is to begin the acquisition phase (initial training for each new skill) in the yard. Only when it is fluent in that environ-

ment do you go into the field to generalize, and even then you will simplify the drills to compensate for the increased difficulty and distractions. So, in this chapter, we will begin with intensive yard work and then provide some guidelines for the transition into the field.

Fetching on Command

In the first stage of training a retrieve—acquisition—we train the dog to fetch an object on command. This means going out to the indicated object, picking it up, returning to the handler, and delivering it to hand. In traditional retriever training, this is accomplished by using R− (see Chapter 1). The handler creates an uncomfortable situation for the dog—usually by pinching her ear or squeezing a dowel between her toes—and when she opens her mouth to protest, he places a dummy between her teeth and releases the pressure. So the dog learns that, to relieve the pain, she needs to grab the dummy. Then, in a gradual process, the dog learns to come forward, take the dummy, hold it, and release it on command.

We use another way. By relying on positive reinforcement (R+)—reinforcing the dog for the correct behavior rather than using pain—we can build an effective response to the "fetch" command through shaping. Here's how to teach the conditioned retrieve, or retrieve on command. As you read through the method, look at the pictures in Figure 6.1 to see how it works with a young retriever.

Before starting to shape a retrieve, review the sections on shaping by successive approximation in Chapter 1, and on criteria setting, reinforcement, and record keeping in Chapters 2 and 3. These are the key concepts that you will use in training the retrieve. Also—and we know this is difficult—hold off on playing fetch with your dog during the time you are working on teaching her to retrieve on command. You need to build up this behavior systematically, and it can be confusing to a dog if the game of fetch and the command "fetch" are going on at the same time. Don't worry: after a few weeks of training, your dog will be an even more enthusiastic fetcher.

If you train the conditioned retrieve properly, all other retrieve work will go very quickly. These exercises are the fundamentals of the retrieve, so don't rush them.

Step 1: Preparing yourself. Get an object to work with. We usually start with an individual-sized plastic water bottle, a fetch stick made of tennis-ball material with a rope on the end, or an appropriately sized retrieving dummy. Hold the object by the neck between the index and middle fingers and the clicker between the index finger and thumb of the left hand. The right hand is free to hand out treats. Start by sitting on the floor with your dog, since that position usually causes her to want to be near you—but be sure to protect your treats!

Step 2: Targeting the object. Start by putting the object in front of the dog's face until she pays it some kind of attention. When first starting, the attention may be as slight as simply looking at the target. The instant she pays attention to the object, C/T. Use the object sparingly as a lure; don't get into the trap of helping the dog too much. However, you'll want to keep your rate of reinforcement high (see Chapter 2), so if the dog is losing interest, put the object a fraction of an inch away from her nose to get her started.

Continue to C/T until the first behavior is solid, and then move to the next level. As a rule of thumb, you can raise your criteria when the dog repeats the behavior correctly four times out of five (80%), with no intervening behaviors (except eating the treat). In other words, the dog targets the object with her nose, looks at you, receives and eats the treat, then immediately targets the object again. A logical progression might be: smell the object, target the object,

paw the object (don't reinforce this too much since it isn't what you ultimately want—perhaps once for doing something different), small push of the object, large push of the object, lift the object with muzzle, tooth accidentally comes in contact with the object, tooth on object purposely, small bite of object, and so on. Each dog will have a different progression; just remember to keep the criteria low enough to result in a high rate of reinforcement. Have a game plan in mind, but be willing to improvise if the dog does something unexpected. (See Chapter 2 for more information on raising criteria and keeping your rate of reinforcement high.)

Once the dog is regularly taking the object in her mouth, introduce a verbal command. We recommend "fetch." Say the word just before the dog moves forward to take the object. After a number of trials (the exact number will depend on the dog), say the word before the dog moves toward the object and see if she begins to move. If so, you can continue to use the verbal command; if not, keep working to solidify the cue by watching the dog carefully and using the word just before the dog's movement. Eventually, it will take hold.

A Digression About Words

Before you move ahead, it's worth thinking a bit about the words you will use for your retrieving commands. Most gun dog trainers use "fetch" to mean "pick up the indicated object and return it to my hand." But in hunting or trial situations, many handlers send their dogs to retrieve on their name. This is really a matter of choice. The advantage of using the dog's name is that it can reduce confusion when there is more than one dog around. The disadvantage is that in pet dog or obedience training, the name is generally used to mean "pay attention to the next command." So using the name for a retrieve command can be confusing to dogs that have been trained to look for another command upon hearing their names.

6.1 The Trained Retrieve

Start with C/T for looking at the dummy ...

... holding the dummy ...

... then targeting the dummy ...

... coming forward to take and hold ...

... taking the dummy in the mouth ...

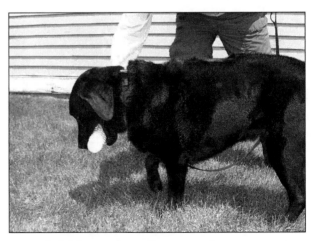

... and picking up from the ground.

Another retrieving command is "back." This is generally used for a blind retrieve (see Chapter 7) and means "go out in the direction you are facing and hunt for something to retrieve." But some handlers use this for marked retrieves as well.

So words matter, but only to the dog! We suggest that you decide at the earliest stage of your training what words you plan to use, and be consistent with them from that day forward. It will make your dog's responses much more solid than if you change them later.

Back to the Conditioned Retrieve

Step 3: Hold (duration). Once you've managed to get the dog's mouth around the object, it's time to start refining the behavior. The logical next step is a hold. When the dog has her mouth around the object, count to one and then C/T. Start with a short interval and gradually work up. You can measure the interval by counting to yourself as quickly as you can. (Learn to be consistent in your counting rhythm.) Holding is usually the most difficult behavior to train and requires patience on the trainer's part. It has been our experience that consistency is the key; the initial hold will be only a fraction of a second. If your criteria are consistent, the dog will learn much quicker. By the time you are up to a fast 10-count, start mixing it up; don't always increase the length of the hold or the dog will know what's expected and there will come a point when the treat is no longer worth it. However, if sometimes she's treated for holding it for a 2-count and sometimes for a 20-count, she'll be more likely to work. This is a variable duration schedule of reinforcement (see Chapter 2).

Step 4: Pickup. Once you've attained a reasonable hold, you can begin to move the object to the ground. When introducing something new, such as a pickup, the dog's behavior will be what determines the criteria. Some dogs will run right over and pick up the object; others will ignore it. You may need to do some intermediate steps first, such as holding the object farther away, then closer to the floor, and so on. If you need to go back to doing a C/T for targeting the object, then do so; the behavior should

get back to where you were quickly, since the dog basically knows it already. Once the dog is reliably picking up the object, if you plan to use a "fetch" command, start introducing it.

Step 5: Carry. Carrying combines the pickup and the hold. Again, dogs will vary in their ability to master this behavior. Just remember to keep the rate of reinforcement high. If your dog doesn't instinctively bring the object back to you, C/T for looking in your direction, then for taking one step in your direction, and so on. The dog may pick up the object, carry it a few steps, then drop it. If she does, count how many steps she's taking (on average) and C/T for that many steps—don't click for fewer—until the behavior is solid. Once it's solid, you can C/T for one or two additional steps until that's solid, and so on. Remember that this is a duration exercise and at some point you need to start mixing it up so she won't know exactly when she'll be treated. You might say "hold it" to reinforce the hold during the carry.

Step 6: Drop. Once your dog is holding the object, you want her to hold it until you indicate otherwise. (Whether you work on this before or after the carry doesn't matter.) Once you've got a reliable hold, start working on the drop. If your dog won't drop the object on command, trade the object for a treat, clicking as she opens her mouth to drop the object. Immediately give the object back; you don't want your dog to think that because she gave it to you, she'll never see it again. If she thinks she'll get it back, she'll be much more likely to drop it. If your dog is reluctant to let go, see Chapter 4 for training a "leave it" command.

Step 7: Take it on the road (generalizing). Once your dog is fluent with the above behaviors, start working with different objects, in different locations, under different circumstances. The final step is to introduce birds (see Chapter 8 for some things to think about when getting your dog used to birds). When generalizing the retrieve, be sure to include a variety of birds. Start with a frozen bird in the living room or backyard, work that until the dog is proficient, then generalize it. Introduce a fresh, thawed bird, work until proficient, generalize, and so on. Keep doing this and gradually introduce all types of birds your dog might encounter, including cripples (which you can simulate by clipping the flight wings) and, for flushing dogs, healthy, live birds.

Remember that when you introduce something new, you need to go back, sometimes all the way to the beginning, and work on one aspect of the behavior at a time. The dog will pick up the new behavior much more quickly and solidly than the first behavior because she already knows it at one level; however, it's very important to start at a low level and slowly and systematically bring her up to the level you are aiming for. Trying to short-circuit the process will usually result in a disappointing performance when you least want it—such as in the middle of an important trial when the distractions and excitement levels are very high.

Also, recall from our discussion of learning theory the concepts of external inhibition and latent learning. Sometimes, taking a short break from training will reduce a dog's stress and provide time for that unconscious learning to take place. So remember that skipping a day can often help.

Fluency with the "Fetch" Command

Once your dog is reliably fetching various objects from the ground fairly close to you, it's time to reinforce the "fetch" command through some systematic exercises. A word of warning: these activities are repetitive and can get boring pretty quickly for both you and the dog. Maintaining a high rate of reinforcement will make it more enjoyable. Remember: every time your dog performs correctly, *you* are also being reinforced! Remember to C/T after each successful performance at the beginning, and then gradually move to a variable reinforcement schedule. Also, keep the sessions short and always try to end with something fun.

Remember that for an enthusiastic retriever, the retrieve itself can be a great reinforcer. His behavior will tell you whether that is sufficient, or whether you will need to supplement with other reinforcers. One great idea is to toss a "happy bumper" as a reinforcer for a successful session. A happy bumper is just a fun retrieve in which you throw a dummy for your dog to chase for the sheer fun of it, with no expectation about a sharp return or delivery. As the name implies, its function is to keep your dog happy and feeling reinforced about his work. The happy bumper is a great reinforcer (sometimes even better than a food treat for some dogs), and the only caution is to use it carefully so as not to undermine the disciplined retrieving that your dog is now learning. Finally, feel free to mix in a bird or two from time to time. It's much more fun to fetch birds than those boring dummies!

Chaining

Chaining is the linking of several behaviors together for a single goal. The best way to teach a chain is to teach each behavior, then put them together. The retrieve is a classic example of chaining. The retrieve is made up of several behaviors: stay, take, hold, drop, go out, and recall. We could probably break it down even further, but this will do for illustrative purposes.

You can front-chain or back-chain. There are advantages to each. With front-chaining, you start with the first link in the chain and work each behavior, up to the last link. With back-chaining, you start with the last link in the chain—in the case of the retrieve, it's the drop to hand. The thinking is that by back-chaining, you'll be reinforcing the final behavior more often than any other behavior, thus creating a strong final behavior through a long, robust reinforcement history. You can't always back-chain. In the retrieve, for example, you can't teach the drop until you've taught the take and hold.

When you can, it's better to back-chain. With the retrieve, once you've taught the take, hold, and drop, you can stop reinforcing the take and hold and just reinforce the drop. That way, every time your dog brings the object to you and drops it to hand, she is being reinforced and you are creating a stronger behavior. You can work on distance, distraction, and difficulty while still reinforcing the drop to hand.

Of course, this is what most retriever trainers are doing already. We just want to bring the concept to your attention so you can use it in other situations and be more conscious of helpful training techniques. Whenever possible, incorporate the more difficult behaviors into a chain in which the final behavior has a very strong reinforcement history.

Exercises

The first exercise introduces your dog to fetching an object from the ground, by your side, from a position of motion. It's an essential building block in training your dog to find something that she has not seen fall. Begin by dropping some dummies in a line on the ground, at least 10 feet apart. Let your dog watch you do this. Walk your dog forward and, as you approach each dummy, give the "fetch" cue. If you have done a solid job on the conditioned retrieve, the dog should move forward, as in Figure 6.2, pick up the dummy, bring it back to you, and hold it until told to release. (If not, then go back and do some more work on the conditioned retrieve. One of the benefits of the walking fetch is that it can reveal deficiencies in earlier training that are easily corrected, without setting the training timetable back very far.) After you take the first dummy, you can drop it on the ground for a subsequent pass. Then walk the dog forward to a second dummy, and repeat the process. The first few times, use only two or three dummies, do one or two repetitions of the drill, and end with a happy bumper or another positive experience for your dog. You can then expand to a larger number; building up to half a dozen bumpers will give you a good foundation for the next step.

6.2 Walking Fetch

Pickups in a row.

C'mon Back!

If your dog tries to pick up the bumper and run, you can use a check cord as pictured in Figure 6.3 to keep control while you coax the pup back. (See Chapter 5 for information on check cords and other equipment.) If the dog is consistently running away with dummies, you need to take a break and reinforce the recall command. Give the dog a dummy to hold, move a short distance away, and give a recall. Reinforce her return generously. Then gradually extend the distance to 25 to 30 yards. You can then go back and test her willingness to retrieve from a pile and come back to you.

When your dog is consistently picking up a series of bumpers from the ground as you walk, you can begin to extend the distance of the retrieve. Drop several bumpers on the ground in a pile. Walk your dog up to about 20 feet from the pile and toss a bumper to mark the pile's position. Then send your dog with the cue "fetch." This helps the dog learn to go out on command (avoiding refusals or "no go's"). It reassures the dog that, whenever you send her, there will be something to retrieve.

6.3 Pile Work

Young dog on a check cord.

When your dog returns with the dummy, have her drop it in your hand, mark the behavior with your clicker or bridge word, and bring her around so she is facing the pile. Send her to the pile again. Do two or three repetitions. At this point, think about the command you plan to use when you send your dog to retrieve in the field or in tests. (See "A Digression About Words," earlier in this chapter.) Be sure to be consistent with your cues; doing so will help your dog as she progresses to more challenging tasks.

Once your dog is reliably returning a dummy from a pile that is close by, you can begin to extend the distance. Toss the first dummy and, after you send your dog, take about 10 steps back while she is on her way to the pile. Then send her a second time from the new position. You can do this several times and, over several sessions, build up to where the dog is consistently going out to a pile 30 to 40 yards away.

After you've worked through these exercises, your dog has learned to go out a considerable distance on your cue, pick up what she finds there, bring it back, and deliver it to you. When you and your dog have reached this level, you are ready to do some real retrieving. Recall that, when working on distance, we recommend that you mix it up so you are not always increasing distance. The dog will figure this

out and be less cooperative than if you use some variety. Have an average distance in mind—say 30 yards—and work on that most of the time. But sometimes use 10 yards, sometimes 35 yards, sometimes 20 yards. This keeps it interesting and motivating for the dog.

Mark!

If you have made it through the tedium of walking fetch and pile work, both you and your dog deserve to have some fun. You've built a strong foundation of obedience and taught your dog that fetching is not only an exciting game, it's also a reinforcing job. It's time to take these skills to the next level.

For this stage, it's useful to have some help. While having the dog fetch things that you toss is great fun and helpful in training, that isn't what the dog will find in the field or in a trial. In those situations, a bird will fall or be thrown at a distance—not by you—and the dog will have to mark the bird's fall and bring it back on command. So we recommend you recruit an assistant, or invest in some equipment, to help you out. (Some people refer to the assistant as a "bird boy," regardless of age or gender; we prefer "assistant," or "helper," or better yet, "friend.")

6.4 Bird Boy Drill

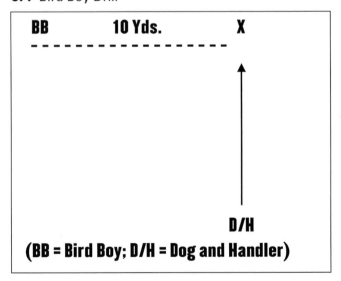

To help the dog learn marking, have your assistant walk out about 10 yards in front and 10 yards to the side of where you and your dog are lined up (see Figure 6.4). Have him toss a dummy (and occasionally a bird) so it lands about 10 yards directly in front of you and the dog. As the assistant tosses the dummy, have him blow a duck call, say something to get the dog's attention, or make a quacking noise. Give your dog the cue "mark!" That's a cue to look out toward the area where a bird is expected to fall. When the dummy lands, send your dog using the retrieving cue you have chosen. Reinforce generously when she comes back to you and delivers the dummy.

There are a couple of things that can go wrong at this stage. One is that the dog won't get the idea of picking up something that another person tosses. Another is that the dog may try to take the dummy to your assistant rather than bring it back to you. After all, that's what the cue means: pick up the indicated object and bring it to the person who tossed it.

When you run into these problems, a single technique will often fix both of them. Instead of having your assistant out in front of you and your dog, have him stand right next to you at first. If your dog is accustomed to bringing back a bumper that you toss to a pile, there's a good chance that she will pursue one tossed from next to you. You may have to step in front of your assistant to intercept the dog on her return, and C/T generously after you take the dummy from her. You can then gradually change your assistant's position, having him move a few feet farther out and to the side each session. After several sessions, your dog will probably retrieve a bumper tossed out to 10 yards or so with your assistant in the desired position.

The next step is to gradually increase the distance of the retrieve. To do this, first send the dog out to about 10 yards; then, as she is heading out, move

back about 5 yards. The next few times, send her from 15 yards, then move back another 5 yards to 20. That's probably enough for a first session, but over time you can gradually increase the distance to 50 yards or more, and eventually to more than 100 yards. Remember: mix it up! Don't always make each trial harder.

If you can't find someone to be your assistant, you can instead use a mechanical remote dummy launcher. There are several good models available that you can trigger by remote control (see Chapter 5 for photos and more information). Most of them toss a dummy or bird 25 yards or more and have a built-in duck call or other sound that you can also control remotely. Some throw only a single object, while others can do multiple launches. (Be careful about the dimensions; your launcher, dog, and other equipment might not fit in your vehicle!)

Bang! It's a Bird!

We recommend that you condition your dog to be comfortable with gunshots before you reach this point. You can, in fact, begin this process of "classical conditioning" quite early. (See Chapter 8 for a detailed discussion of gun conditioning.) Begin by making sharp noises such as handclaps around your puppy, always followed by a treat. Gradually increase the noise level. To get the dog used to gunshots, begin at a distance and gradually come closer so that the shot is louder. Have your assistant work up from .22 caliber blanks to 12-gauge shotgun poppers, always monitoring your dog to ensure that she is comfortable with the noise level and giving a treat after each sound. Have your assistant gradually work his way closer to you and the dog. You can then introduce gunshots from your position, again starting with .22s and working up to 12-gauge. Using a shoulder-fired dummy launcher can be particularly helpful at this point (described in Chapter 5).

Extending Distance: The Traditional Approach ...

Most traditional trainers believe it's important, when extending the distance, to move the position from which you and the dog start, not the place where the dummy falls. They argue that a dog that has once retrieved from a particular area will instinctively return to that area to hunt. So if the dog has to run through the area of a previous "fall," there's a good chance she will stop there and not go on to the farther bumper. In the traditional view, it's possible to train a dog to run past a previous fall but too difficult for this stage of training, so it's better to avoid the problem. However, you can prevent this problem if your assistant always tosses to the same area, and you and your dog move to increase the distance.

... And an Alternative

Other experienced animal trainers, including Bob Bailey, have a different view. Bob indicated in a personal communication that it is often better to train the animal from the beginning to go through the spot associated with a previous target. This is based on the idea that it is a mistake to create any habit of this sort; therefore, don't ever throw or place the dummy in the same spot twice in a row. They believe this will create a stronger performance in the long run, although it may take longer to "proof." In his training classes, Jim, one of the authors, has used the traditional approach, and it has worked. But we also believe that there is great sense to what Bailey says, and are open to his method as well. One of the other authors, Susan (who studied with Bailey), is experimenting with his approach with her own dog. We encourage some of you to try it, and to let us know if you are successful.

To repeat a point made in Chapter 1, we do not recommend "flooding" as a technique to condition a dog to gunshot. Flooding, you'll recall, involves repeatedly exposing the dog to an uncomfortable stimulus in the hope that she will become habituated to this. Although this technique can be effective, we think it is too tricky for anyone other than the most experienced behaviorists to use. The risk of serious emotional damage to the dog is too great, and we strongly recommend the systematic approach outlined above.

Overcoming Inhibition: The Traditional Approach ...

Most books on retriever training recommend a correction-based approach to overcoming poor performance. For example, Mike Lardy, in his article "Guidelines for Corrections" (*The Retriever Journal,* October/November 1998, pp. 54–56), recommends giving "corrections" (a stimulus from an electronic collar) for a mistake that stems from what he calls lack of effort, matching the intensity and duration of the stimulus to the handler's perception of the severity of the infraction. He then recommends simplifying the task and trying again.

... And an Alternative

Our view is that we should not assume that a dog's mistakes stem from lack of effort. As believers in Morgan's Canon of Parsimony (see Chapter 1), we think there are simpler explanations. For example:

- The cue was unclear, perhaps because of low volume or a sloppy hand signal.
- The behavior is not under stimulus control (see Chapter 4); that is, there is not enough reinforcement history.

(continues)

... And an Alternative *(continued)*

- The behavior has not been "proofed" (generalized) for the level of distraction or difficulty.
- The trainer lumped the criteria, rather than splitting them into more manageable steps.
- The trainer is unaware that backward steps (i.e., external inhibition) are normal components of the learning process.

We agree that simplifying is the best approach, and we also believe that positive punishment (P+) is not appropriate in most cases. Instead, we suggest you interrupt the unwanted behavior before it becomes intrinsically reinforcing, and try again. However, if the dog has been well trained in a particular task and fails to perform it several times, P– may be helpful. We find that a brief "time-out" in the crate or the truck can be useful. If it is not, it's time for you to take a break and rethink your training approach.

Once you have gotten your dog used to the sound of the gunshot, you will convert the sound from a noise to a cue. Give your assistant a starter's pistol and some blanks. Then ask him to walk out into position and, just as he tosses the duck, to fire a round. After many repetitions, your dog will learn that the gunshot "predicts" the bird. It will not only help her to be more comfortable with the noise, but also to look out and mark the fall. Many of the remote launchers have slots and firing pins for blanks of various calibers and noise levels.

Building Drive in Your Dog

We hope that your dog is now enthusiastically retrieving on command out to a considerable distance. If so, you are lucky, and you are to be commended for your patient systematic training.

But even the best-trained retriever is likely to have an occasional attack of "external inhibition," that unexplained failure to perform tasks that you know have been thoroughly trained (see Chapter 1). Sometimes your dog just seems to lack the desire to retrieve. If your dog seems to lack drive, several methods can help you build it up.

Steadiness: The Traditional Approach ...

Many US trainers believe that you should wait until your dog is enthusiastically going out 50 or more yards to retrieve and is reliably delivering to you before you begin enforcing some steadiness. To enforce steadiness in this approach, you need to first ensure that your dog has a reliable sit-stay when you are some distance away. Sit your dog beside you, give a "stay" command, and toss a bumper out a few yards. Then, instead of sending the dog for it, go out and get it yourself. Do this once, and then let the dog pick up the next dummy. Repeat the cycle and end the session. In future sessions, gradually increase the distance or the time you are away. Also increase the number of times that you pick up the dummy and reduce the number that she retrieves, until she is retrieving only about a third of the time and you are picking up dummies out to about 25 yards on the other tosses.

Once you and your dog have mastered this drill, you can have your assistant start to pick up bumpers that he tosses while you keep your dog in a stay. And you can also ask your dog to hold a stay before being sent for a tossed bumper. Repeat this drill in each training session to reinforce the concept.

(continues)

... And an Alternative (continued)

Another approach that has been successful with other species is to teach all of the required components of a complex behavior from the beginning. The reason for this is that it is much harder to change an established behavior than to install a new behavior. We believe that, with proper positive reinforcement, a dog can be steady from the beginning of his training in retrieving. Our thinking is that the dog's drive is both instinctive and a function of the high rate of reinforcement used in fetch training. The more difficult component of retrieving is teaching a dog not to retrieve, that is, to be steady. By diligently training a sit-stay, and by using the privilege of retrieving as a reinforcer, you can train steadiness as an inherent component of retrieving from the time the dog first learns to fetch objects from the ground. This is the approach used by most British trainers, who work first on steadiness and solid obedience before introducing birds and longer retrieves. We invite you to try it and report your experience.

The most basic approach to build drive is to ensure that the retrieve is always highly reinforcing for the dog. Dogs do what works, so they are more likely to repeat a behavior that is consistently and generously reinforced. This is where you really need to know your dog. Be sure that you are using the most attractive reinforcement, and keep your rate of reinforcement very high. Know whether your dog is most motivated by food treats (and which ones), by a belly rub, a happy bumper, or another chance to retrieve. And be alert for reinforcers that can pop up in the environment, like a short swim or chance to romp with another dog after a training session. (This is the Premack Principle—using a high probability behavior to reinforce a low probability behavior.) Always end training on a happy note, with a high-value reinforcer, and with your dog panting for more.

You may also find that your dog gets bored with retrieving the same old canvas dummy every time. Have her retrieve a variety of objects, including birds. When your training birds deteriorate, you can take off some feathers and stick them in a dummy to make it more attractive. You can also buy duck and quail scent to inject into the dummy. Many dogs like Dead Fowl Trainers (see Chapter 5). These rubber replicas simulate the weight of a duck or other game bird and have a swivel neck to imitate a dead fowl. They can build enthusiasm and improve your dog's hold on actual birds. In our experience, a bird, or something very much like one, does wonders to build retrieving drive.

Finally, you can return to your puppy training games to improve enthusiasm. Remember the game in which you toss one toy down the hall and then toss a second as your dog runs back with the first? You can do the same thing with your older dog to reinforce her drive. In their book *Schutzhund Obedience Training in Drive*, Sheila Booth and Gottfried Dildei recommend playing the game with two sections of flexible radiator hose, teasing the dog by wiggling the hoses to get her excited about the chase. Some trainers we know have used this technique to teach the conditioned retrieve, by gradually shaping the dog to come closer and deliver the first hose before going for the second.

Steady!

Training steadiness in the field is one area in which many American and British trainers differ. This reflects the differences in hunting styles and field sports. The rules for the American Kennel Club (AKC) Junior Hunter test specify that a junior dog does not have to be steady but can be gently restrained before being sent for the bird. Steadiness at the line is not required until the Senior Hunter level.

Trainers in the United Kingdom incorporate steadiness into the earliest phases of training. British hunting often involves many dogs that "beat" (walk in a line with other dogs and people to push game toward the guns) and "pick up" (take station with other dogs behind the guns and retrieve when directed). Thus control and steadiness are essential. British trials are structured to reflect "an ordinary day's shooting." The United Kingdom's Gundog Club, for example, requires retrievers at the beginning level to hold a two-minute sit-stay with the handler 20 yards away. In general, we prefer the British approach to steadiness. But this is an individual matter and depends on the trainer's goals as well as location. (See the box on page 63–64 for a discussion of alternative views about when to incorporate steadiness into the retrieving sequence.)

Put It Here, Pup

We're not talking about shaking paws, but about delivery to hand. If you've been scrupulous about your training so far, your dog should be coming back to you and waiting for you to take the dummy or bird from him. If not, get a newspaper, roll it up, and hit yourself on the head with it! You need to go back to the conditioned retrieve and retrain the hold and deliver. Don't take a shortcut; this is of vital importance if you want to have edible birds or to pass the hunt test.

Once again, there are differing styles and training goals to consider. In competitive obedience, dogs are usually trained to present the object from the front or sitting position, directly before the handler. British trainers also favor this approach.

Many American trainers have the dog come to heel first before taking the bird. This not only looks classy but also enables the trainer to line the dog up for a subsequent retrieve. (Multiple retrieves are common in US tests and trials.) If you have trained your dog to complete her recalls by sitting in front of you, try luring her around your back with a treat and having her sit before you C/T. When this behavior is solid, you can fade the lure and just use a hand signal to beckon her around to your side.

(You can introduce a verbal command at this point or after the next step, whichever you prefer.) Next, have her perform this sequence with a dummy, first coming to the front, then around to heel. You can then begin to use the "heel" command (verbal or hand signal) as she is approaching. Eventually, you can fade the command, and the dog will return to the heel position automatically. As always, when training a series of behaviors, use a high rate of reinforcement, and be prepared to simplify if she seems confused.

If you want to be really fancy, you can train a "flip finish," in which the dog comes to your heel side directly and "flips" around into the heel position. The principle is the same; just use the lure to get that motion instead of having her come around your back. This doesn't affect anything at all in the field or in a test, but you and your dog can feel special if she does it.

Dogs must heel off-lead to the line at the Senior and Master hunt test levels in the United States. In the United Kingdom's Gundog Club program, dogs must heel off-lead at the Junior level and do their entire test off-lead at the Intermediate level! There's nothing in the rules about coming to the heel position to deliver at any level, but judges seem to want it, and there is one good reason to train it, which is for multiple retrieves. Most trainers want the dog to come to heel and be lined up for the next bird, so that you don't have to turn her around to head off in the right direction.

Distance and Doubles

If you have followed the exercises in the book so far and now have a dog that reliably goes out 50 or more yards, picks up a bird or dummy, returns to the heel position, and holds it until you take it, congratulations! You have a trained, working retriever on your hands. What next? Two other goals that you can pursue before you head out to your favorite hunting preserve are: increasing the distance your dog goes, and training "double retrieves."

It's easy to increase distance: gradually move back the imaginary line from which you send your dog over a number of training sessions. The difficulty comes when we try to move farther from the fall than the dog can handle. As with all aspects of retriever training, increase distance gradually; the dog should be thoroughly reliable at the shorter distance before you send him out farther. Remember your record keeping and maintain good notes on the number of sets, trials, and success rates. As a rule of thumb, increase distance no more than 10 yards per session. Even with this modest rate of increase, it will be only a few weeks before your dog is going 100 or more yards. And remember, even though you have a particular distance as your goal, mix it up, doing some trials shorter, some farther out, but most at your target distance.

Toby's First WC

The first time Jim, one of the authors, ran Toby in a Working Certificate (WC) test, the pair didn't make it past the land retrieve, because Toby found his bird very quickly and then decided to take it for a walk after dropping it a couple of times!

So it was back to the yard for Jim and Toby. First, they revisited the conditioned retrieve, putting emphasis on a good pickup. They did this by using differential reinforcement of excellent behavior (DRE), as described in Chapter 2, combined with a keep-going signal (KGS) as described in Chapter 4.

The other task was to strengthen Toby's recall. Jim used Leslie Nelson's "Really Reliable Recall" method, which is described in an excellent video available from Tawzer Dog Videos. Essentially it involves reinforcing the dog continuously with high-value reinforcers for at least 30 seconds, so that the "recall" command becomes classically conditioned to predict an association with a real jackpot. This technique results in greatly increased effectiveness.

Always remember that control diminishes, and distractions increase, with distance. So we urge you to be patient, reinforce each increment of distance generously, and not to be reluctant to move to a shorter distance and stay there for a while to ensure that your dog is solid before moving on.

Double retrieves can be a lot of fun for you and your dog and can build enthusiasm as well as steadiness. A double requires that your dog watch one bird or dummy fall, then shift to another direction and watch a second one fall. You send your dog to pick up and deliver the second dummy or bird, and then send him in for the first. We call the first bird to fall the "memory bird" and the second one the "go bird." In advanced retriever training, hunting, and trials, multiple marks—up to four birds—are common.

6.5 Double Retrieves: Method One

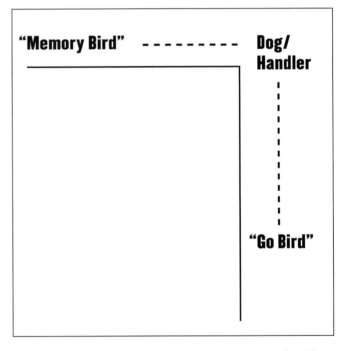

Some trainers advocate waiting on training doubles until the dog has had significant work on single retrieves in the field. We can see the advantages and disadvantages of waiting. We've found that dogs and handlers often reach a plateau and it's fun and helpful to introduce a new skill to spice things up.

Whichever style you choose—training doubles after extending the distance of singles or waiting until the dog is solid on singles in the field—the following is our suggested approach.

There are two ways to begin doubles, depending on the configuration of your property. If you have a yard on two adjacent sides of your house (see Figure 6.5), throw the memory bird on one side of the house, then turn your dog to face down the other side and throw the go bird. Receive the go bird at your side, so the dog is facing the memory bird, and send her again. When she returns with the memory bird, C/T. Keep up a high rate of reinforcement until she returns both birds smoothly. When you are consistently successful working next to the house, begin to back up so she has to run more of her pattern in the open, away from the wall. Over a number of sessions, she will learn to come right back to you with the go bird, even in an open area.

If you don't have the ideal yard, you can begin doubles in any open area of 50 yards or so. Stand in the middle (see Figure 6.6) with the dog at your side, and toss a dummy out in front. Heel your dog around until you are facing in the opposite direction of the first dummy, and toss the second. Send the dog for the second dummy; when she turns around, she will have to pass you if she wants to go to the first. Intercept her and take the dummy before you let her retrieve the memory bird. Over time, you can make the angle smaller until she can do doubles that have less than 90 degrees between them. As always, take it slowly and, if the dog seems confused, open the angle back up. Continue to work at the dog's level of comfort before trying closer doubles again.

6.6 Double Retrieves: Method Two

```
"Memory  - - - - -  Dog/ - - - - -  "Go Bird"
  Bird"              Handler
```

Decoys and Other Paraphernalia

When you take your dog hunting or to a test or trial, she will have to contend with many distractions. She will see decoys, guns, blinds, boats, field stools, gear bags, other people, and dogs. It is important that you introduce your dog systematically to each of these distractions—one at a time—before she has to confront them all in a new setting.

Let's take decoys as an example. If your dog hasn't seen one before, during a test she's as likely to retrieve the decoy as the bird. That will get her dismissed from a hunt test!

To introduce decoys, begin with just a couple of them. Start in the yard, in a place your dog knows well, with few distractions. Put the decoys right in front of you. Let her sniff them, but do not let her pick them up. If she tries, use your "leave it" command, or if necessary, a no reward marker (a verbal cue for extinction, rather than a punisher). Have your assistant stationed at a fairly short distance. It's best to begin these drills at no more than half the distance that your dog has successfully run for retrieves in the past. Instruct him to make an exciting noise and then throw a dummy or, even better, a bird. If your dog shows interest in the decoys as she returns with the bird, get her attention with enthusiastic noises or a treat if necessary. C/T with a high-value reinforcer when she delivers. Repeat this several times in the first session.

Over time, you will vary two factors: the number of decoys and their distance from you. Very gradually, move the decoys closer to the area of the fall. If the dog diverts to the decoys, stop her, move them back closer to you, and try again. Once your dog can handle a couple of decoys at a distance, you can increase the number, one at a time, until she can run through a large spread with confidence.

In keeping with our positive reinforcement philosophy, nowhere in this process do we "correct" the dog. Even if she stopped to sniff the decoy, in our opinion the dog did nothing to warrant a correction. We are trying to extinguish the behavior of going to the decoys. Extinction will occur if a behavior is not reinforced (see Chapter 1). So over time, if the dog receives no positive consequence for going to the dummies, the behavior will disappear. The dog will become habituated to the decoys; they will simply be an unremarkable part of the environment. Training this can be a little tricky. We need to ensure that we are not inadvertently reinforcing the behavior by giving the dog attention. Even negative attention such as saying "No!" can be reinforcing. We also need to interrupt the behavior before it becomes intrinsically reinforcing, for example if the dog licks or chews the decoys. So good timing and gentle handling are essential.

We assume that if the dog didn't perform as we asked, the problem is either with our training or with the environment. It follows that the solution is to take a step back in training or make the environment less distracting, and then gradually move forward. As our colleague Steve Rafe is fond of saying, there never seems to be enough time to do it correctly the first time, but if we are methodical, we will save more time in the long run.

Just start with a simple setup, and gradually change the distance and number of distractions as the dog becomes more confident. Whenever you change one factor, such as distance, it's important to simplify the other factors so the dog only has to deal with one new thing at a time.

If you aspire to hunt testing with your dog, you will have to get the dog used to numerous decoys and to the distractions of the test site. You can make recordings at a test if you want to, and play them while you train, so that your dog gets used to the noise. Give your dog experience in walking nicely to a holding blind, staying there for some time, and then heeling to the line from which you will send her to retrieve. Your dog will also have to tolerate you holding a shotgun; if you don't want to spend the money for one, you can buy a wooden "handler's gun," or even use a stick of shotgun length. It's also worth getting the dog used to retrieving for you when you are sitting down or from a boat. You never know what tricks the judges will pull!

In sum, the mantra for distraction training is: "One thing at a time, slowly."

Into the Field

After following the training instruction up to this point of the book, you'll have completed the first phase of your yard work. Of course, you will return to the yard when you introduce new concepts to your dog, but if you've done your training thoroughly so far, you are ready to make the initial transition to the field.

A few words of caution: When you go from the yard to the field, you will almost certainly see deterioration in your dog's performance. The field is full of interesting smells, animals, birds, and maybe other people and dogs as well. For a young hunting dog especially, these distractions can be quite overwhelming. So for your first foray into the field, we recommend that you start with some short single retrieves, thrown by your able assistant or your remote launcher. The distance will depend on the dog's level of training and on the degree of distractions, but if you have been getting retrieves at 50 or more yards in the backyard, 25 yards is a good place to start in the field. (If you don't have 50 yards in your backyard, you can try a ball field or other enclosed area. Maybe there's a park or vacant lot near you where you can train your dog safely on a check cord. Or perhaps you'll just have to make some new friends who have big yards!)

Especially in early training, we recommend that you wear light-colored clothing. While dogs are not, strictly speaking, color blind, they can have difficulty distinguishing between certain colors. For example, they do not easily differentiate between orange and brown or green. So we suggest white or a light tan (and definitely not camouflage) for your first field forays.

We recommend that you develop a written training plan and keep track of your dog's performance in the field. (See the example in Appendix III.) By keeping a systematic record of your field work, you accomplish two important goals: you can identify emerging problems very quickly, and you can determine the dog's previous level of accomplishment so you can quickly decide how to go back and simplify. You can then move ahead deliberately and improve the quality of your dog's field performance.

Common Problems

You might be one of the lucky ones whose dog moves smoothly through the training program without a hitch. But it is more likely that you will run into some problems. Here are some common problems and ways in which we have tackled them.

Hard mouth

A well-bred hunting dog should have a soft mouth but, unfortunately, some really like to crunch down on the bird. This is not good, for obvious reasons. If you are working with a puppy, begin to teach bite inhibition very early. Playing with other puppies is the best way for yours to learn to hold back on her bite. Puppies are great at correcting each other when they get nipped too hard. You can reinforce this by imitating what puppies do. Pet your pup and offer her your hand. When she nips it, if there is significant pressure, let out a yelp as another puppy would. If your dog shows signs that she understood the bite was too hard by backing off or looking at you, continue to pet her. If not, remove your hand and turn away for a few seconds. The P– of removing your attention will probably get through to her after a few repetitions.

At this point, you are teaching the dog to mouth softly, not to stop biting. For a hunting dog this is essential. You do, after all, want her to bite down on the bird hard enough to hold it. If you want to work on not biting people at all, do that after the dog has learned to inhibit her bite. However, we recommend maintaining your dog's bite inhibition throughout her life for her protection by installing and initiating biting games and ensuring that she bites only on cue. By doing that you accomplish several things. You maintain your dog's easy bite in case she is in a position in which she feels she has to bite. Unless in an untenable situation, she will bite people only on cue. Lastly, you still have a game you and your dog enjoy playing, but you are prepared for the bites by wearing protective clothing. Bite inhibition is particularly important for sporting dogs, because they are bred to have a soft mouth. This often means that they do not learn effective bite inhibition as puppies and then, if they are in a position in which they feel

they must bite, they are unable to regulate the severity of the bite.

Once your dog is older than 18 weeks and has her permanent teeth, the pressure of her bite will be difficult to change. But we suggest the following method for using shaping to train a hard-mouthed dog to be gentler with the bird. Do three to five normal retrieves with your dog, and count how many times she chomps down on the bird during each retrieve. For example, suppose that after doing around five retrieves, you determine that she usually chomps about five times. Begin reinforcing (with fabulous, stinky food) for five chomps or less. Do not reinforce for anything over five chomps. Also do not scold her or get upset for more than five chomps; just thank her for the bird and continue the lesson. You'll gradually shape her to not chomp on the bird. This doesn't have to take a long time; it depends on how often and how long you train.

Popping

"Popping" occurs when your dog runs toward the bird, then stops and looks at you rather than picking it up. A dog often start popping in the early stages of learning blind retrieves (see Chapter 7), when the handler begins to stop her with whistle sits on the way to a pile. It may also happen if the dog lacks confidence that she is going the right way, especially if it was hard for her to see the fall of the bird.

At this stage of your dog's training, do not use exercises such as whistle sits during blind retrieve exercises—it's too early to introduce those skills. Waiting on these exercises is one way to prevent popping. Often, we trainers are so impressed by our dogs' performances that we rush things. Blinds are so challenging that sometimes we try to introduce them too early. So if your dog is popping, back up and continue to work on marked retrieves until you have both land and water retrieves very solid—out to at least 100 yards on land and 30 yards on water. Also be sure that you are not inadvertently reinforcing the popping by giving your dog encouragement when she pops. Even negative attention from you can be reinforcing to the dog.

Losing a mark

A problem similar to popping happens when a dog runs toward the area of a fall, begins to hunt, and then gives up and starts to return to the handler. Persistence in hunting is fundamental to success in the field and in tests. There are several ways to approach this issue.

Some handlers train a "find it" command by getting the dog to find things around the house and then transferring the skill to the yard and eventually to the field. You can C/T for successful finds, first of highly visible (or great-smelling) objects close at hand, then of objects that are more difficult to find, and later in more distracting areas. For field work, you can use a cue such as "hunt it up" or "hi lost" for this command.

To sharpen your dog's hunting ability, you can do some structured scent games around the house. Use a porous object such as a napkin or towel. Soak it with a strong scent like lemon juice or dish detergent and hold it in your hand. Have your dog first smell the original scent source and then present the scent-soaked target and cue your dog to "find it." Click and treat when your dog sniffs the target in your hand. When this is reliable (at least 80% correct responses), repeat the exercise with the object on the floor, within your dog's sight. When your dog is fluent at that level, start hiding the object out of sight, and coax him forward. Once he's mastered this, you can add similar objects on the floor and only C/T when your dog touches the scented object. You can then repeat the exercises outdoors, using bird scent.

Another technique is to throw "happy bumpers" in areas of higher cover or multiple scents. Dogs are usually enthusiastic about happy bumpers and often hunt for them more thoroughly.

A final idea, but one that requires some help and the right area, comes from professional trainer Jim Dobbs. He suggests that you set up a situation as follows. Stand with your dog at your side, facing downwind. Have an assistant throw some dirt clods onto the ground a distance away. Send the dog to the area with your retrieve command. Because there is no bird there, the dog will probably run past the

clods. Your assistant then stealthily tosses a bird into that area, while the dog is running farther out. Because the dog is then downwind, she has a good chance of picking up the scent and returning to find the bird. An enthusiastic C/T should help to solidify her good hunting!

Blinking

"Blinking" refers to a dog's refusal to pick up a bird that he has located. This can occur for several reasons. There may be new distractions in the area that have captured the dog's attention. If you are using thawed, previously frozen birds, they may begin to decompose after being thawed and refrozen several times. Many dogs are reluctant to pick them up. In addition, dogs that have been trained primarily on frozen birds may not want to pick up a freshly killed bird, or especially a cripple that is still moving. Blinking can also occur when the distance of the retrieve is much farther than the dog's demonstrated capability. Your control diminishes with the distance between you and the dog, and she may be inclined to "do her own thing" at a great distance.

A related problem is chewing or licking a bird. This can occur especially with damaged birds, where blood or moisture is present. The taste is just too good to ignore!

The approach to resolving both of these problems is the same, and one you are familiar with by now. Go back to the trained retrieve and solidify the "fetch" command with a variety of tried and true items, then use the problem bird. If the dog understands that "fetch" really means "pick it up now," she will promptly retrieve on your command. Then return to a distance at which the dog has reliably retrieved in the past and work outward very gradually, waiting for a success rate of at least 80% before extending the distance. If you feel it would help, you can have your dog retrieve a combination of known and novel items in the field. This solidifies the retrieve under field conditions before introducing birds. Be sure that the birds you are using are in good condition. Finally, do not begin to introduce shot flyers until your dog is very consistent first on thawed birds and then on recently killed ones.

Water Retrieves

Retrieving on water combines two skills: retrieving and swimming. Our hope is that our dogs will take to both retrieving and swimming naturally. But, as is the case with the trained retrieve, it's a good idea to be systematic in training our dogs to be comfortable in the water.

Just as you can do puppy retrieves to test and reinforce the retrieving instinct, you can also introduce puppies to water early. Take your pup to a pond or slowly flowing stream when she is 10 to 12 weeks old. See if she goes in on her own. If not, don your boots or wading shoes and plunge in yourself. Entice her to the water's edge with handclapping, a squeaky toy, or treats. Reinforce her for any foray into the water. Gradually, over a period of days, bring her out to swimming depth. Stay close to provide praise and reinforcement, and keep the sessions short; swimming is a strenuous activity.

Another word of caution: pay close attention to the air and water temperature. Wait, if possible, until the water is 60 degrees or warmer before you try to immerse your pup. Even with an older dog, it's a good idea to begin your water training when the pond is 50 degrees or higher. After some experience, dogs—especially those with double coats like Labs and Chessies—can handle cold and icy water, but you don't want to risk having your dog balk at water work because of a temperature shock early on.

Some dogs don't care to swim but will enthusiastically chase an object that is thrown into the water. Whether or not this is the case with your dog, you can use a happy bumper to build your dog's drive for water work. Start by tossing the bumper near the water's edge, gradually moving to shallow water, then, after a time, to swimming depth.

If you can find a calm body of water, with little shoreline vegetation and few other distractions (such as dead fish), your early training will progress more smoothly than in an overgrown pond or a river with a strong current. When you have identified a good training area, begin to work on a serious water retrieve. Start close-in with an easily retrieved item such as a smaller bumper, and gradually extend the distance. Remember that swimming retrieves are much more demanding; even if your dog is doing land retrieves at 100 yards plus, she may find water retrieves challenging. Also, be aware that when your dog is swimming, her eyes are just above water level and she may have difficulty judging distances—another reason to begin close-in and move out very slowly. Once you've got good distance with an easy item, start over—close to shore—with a more difficult item such as a larger bumper.

You may find that your dog enjoys being in the water so much that she wants to play rather than retrieve. If so, back up to shallower water, and be sure that your trained retrieve is solid. Use a high rate of reinforcement for successful retrieves and work patiently and systematically.

Retrieving that stops at the water's edge

Another common problem is the dog that swims out and back enthusiastically, but stops at the shoreline, drops the bird or bumper, and shakes on the return. To combat this, you will need to get a little wet yourself. Wade a few feet into the water and meet your dog on the return, take the bird, and then C/T. Do this a number of times until the dog is reliably delivering to you before she stops and shakes. Then back up a step or two and repeat the process. Proceed gradually until the dog is all the way out of the water, generously reinforcing every successful delivery. After many repetitions, you can try cueing her to return to heel.

Many handlers also teach their dogs to shake off water on command. You can do this by "capturing" the behavior. You can start in the house by brushing your dog—almost all dogs shake after being brushed, so you can easily control the circumstances and environment. Give a few brush strokes, then, with clicker and treats ready, stop brushing. As soon as your dog shakes, C/T. After doing this for several sets (10 to 20 trials), start adding a cue just before she shakes, such as "shake" or a hand signal such as wiggling your hand. Repeat the exercise with the cue several times, and then try giving the cue without brushing the dog. Once this behavior is on cue, take it to the water! When your dog finishes a play session in the water, watch closely for her to shake. When she does, C/T. After several repetitions, introduce the cue just before she begins. Eventually, you should be able to give the cue and she will shake on your command. You can then begin to back-chain the retrieve, deliver, and shake commands in that order. (See Chapter 4 to learn how to get a behavior under stimulus control.)

Cheating and bank running

Dogs are masters at conserving energy. And they know that swimming is more strenuous than running. So they often will take an indirect path to a water retrieve, staying on dry land for as long as possible before getting in the water. If you use your dog for hunting only, this may not be a big deal. After all, you also want your dog to conserve her energy for a long day's hunt.

In hunt tests and field trials, however, "cheating" (not taking a direct line to a mark) and "bank running" (avoiding water and staying on land) can lead to marking down or even disqualification. Our friend Tom Reese, who is training his standard poodle, Wick, at the Master Hunter level, has suggested the following approach to eliminating bank running. He developed his technique for Wick, who already knows "handling" (changing direction on Tom's hand), so it is suitable for advanced dogs, but you can start at any time.

The essence is to train your dog to stop on a whistle command and follow your hand signals. So when she starts to divert to land, you blow your whistle and "cast" her back into the water. Training these commands is described in the next chapter.

Another technique was described by one of the members of the PositiveGunDogs Yahoo Group discussion list. She saw another handler direct his flat-coated retriever back into the water by yelling "swim!" He explained that from the time the dog had been a pup, he called out that word every time the dog entered the water, so it became a cue, with the pleasure of swimming being the reinforcement for the behavior. Eventually, it became a reliable command the handler could use to send the dog back into the water if attempting to run the bank!

Your Trained Retriever

When you have diligently followed the sequence we've outlined, using plenty of R+, you will have reached the "maintenance" stage. At this stage, your dog reliably retrieves marks at moderate distances on land and in the water. She will stay steady until sent, mark the fall, hunt efficiently, and pick up a bird promptly. She will return directly to you—by land or water—and deliver the bird to your hand. When you have reached this stage, you can be very proud of her accomplishments, and yours! Continue working to keep her skills sharp and enjoy each session in the field.

If your dog hasn't reached this standard of perfection, you have the tools to address problems before they become too serious. With a positive attitude and positive training methods, it won't be long before your dog goes on her first hunt or runs her first test.

Chapter 7

Blind Retrieves

Where's That Dang Bird?

The day will come when your dog has to find a bird that he didn't see fall. Maybe you and your friends are hunting and down multiple birds, some in a direction away from where the dog is looking. Maybe you wing one and it flies out of sight before dropping. Or maybe you've lost a bird in training and know only approximately where it is. When this happens, you will be grateful if your dog can do a blind retrieve.

Blind retrieves require an advanced set of skills from both you and your dog. You need to have your dog's confidence in your judgment and directions, be able to send him effectively toward the blind, and stop him and redirect him if he gets off track. Even if your dog has a strong ability to mark the fall of a bird and retrieve it, he won't be able to find a "cold blind" the first time. To develop this ability takes patient, systematic training. You will need to go back and incorporate all of the stages of learning: acquisition, fluency, generalization, and maintenance.

Training Systems

Several fine systems are available that teach dogs to do blind retrieves and other advanced field work. They contain step-by-step drills to help you and your dog master the necessary skills in a systematic and effective way. Among the professional American retriever trainers who have developed training systems are John and Amy Dahl, Jim and Phyllis Dobbs, Evan Graham, and Mike Lardy. These trainers, and other professionals, owe much to the late Rex Carr, who first described an integrated approach to retriever training. We also like the approach outlined in a set of "broadsheets" authored by British trainer Eric Begbie. All of these procedures are described in pamphlets, books, and videos, some of which are listed in Appendix I.

What we like about these systems is that they do a good job of splitting training goals into logical, easily mastered criteria. Thus, they can be adapted—with some effort on your part—to clicker training. We like the approach used by our colleague Tom Reese in training his standard poodles as retrievers. He worked closely with a traditional trainer who helped him determine what to train (the criteria steps), while Tom figured out how to train using positive methods.

While these systems are very well constructed, and have developed many high-performing dogs, they all (except Begbie's) rely on the use of force and punishment, including electronic collars. So we have tried to draw on the work of these professionals, substituting positive training methods for those based on avoidance and correction. In this chapter, we present some of the basics of blind retrieves, but we also recommend that you look at the professionals' books and videos for more detailed information on drills to reinforce your dog's training. With the information we supply, we expect that you will be able to modify those drills to incorporate positive training methods.

A few words of caution: most professional gun dog trainers, and experienced amateurs, recommend that you pick one of the methods and stick to it, rather than mixing elements from two or more. We think this is good advice. The programs all have a logical sequence, and we believe that following one diligently and consistently will produce the best results. In this regard, we urge you to pay close attention to the principles of criteria setting and record keeping in Chapters 2 and 3.

What we describe below is a series of basic exercises that are broadly consistent with the major professional systems. These will get you started, but for more advanced work in the field or in field trials, look carefully at the programs of the Dahls, the Dobbs, Graham, Lardy, and others.

Basic Training for Blind Retrieves

The blind retrieve consists of three separate behaviors. The first is "taking a line," in which the retriever runs out on command in the direction indicated by the handler. This can be directly toward the area of the fall, or in another direction if there are obstacles the handler must direct the dog around. The second is a "whistle stop" or "whistle sit," a command to the dog to stop at a distance, turn around, sit, and look to the handler for the next command. The third behavior is "casting," directing the dog with voice and hand signals to run in a new direction, either to the side or back from his sitting position. The handler combines whistle sits and casts to "handle" the dog to the area of the fall, where the dog's hunting instincts take over and he finds the bird. (In US hunt tests, the handler must direct the dog all the way to the bird; in British trials and in everyday hunting this precision is usually not necessary if the dog has a strong hunting instinct.)

Blinds can be on land, in water, or in a combination of both environments. In this chapter, we will concentrate on land blinds and offer some suggestions for working on water blinds. You can find more detailed recommendations if you study the various training systems mentioned earlier. In any case, when training blinds, remember your record keeping, as always.

Lining

The "lining" command cues the dog to leave the handler and run directly away until given another command. Taking a line requires a lot of faith on the part of your dog. He has to believe that if you send him in a particular direction, there will be something there to retrieve. And it also requires that he understand what direction you want him to go! Dogs don't necessarily realize that if we point or look in a certain direction they should go that way. We have to teach them. Here's a way to begin.

7.1 Sight Blinds

Step 1: Throw a dummy while your dog watches.

Step 2: Heel your dog back to the line and send. Gradually extend distance.

If your dog is solid on his pile work, that is, if he reliably retrieves dummies or birds from a pile out to 50 yards or more, then you can begin to teach lining in a more formal sense. A good way to start the transition is to give your dog some "sight blind" drills (see Figure 7.1). As the name implies, these drills combine elements of marking and blind retrieves. To begin, pick a line from which you will send your dog. Walk with him out a short distance and toss several dummies in front of you so he can see them fall. Say the cue "dead bird" or another word of your choice as you toss them. (This will eventually become a "discriminative stimulus" that signals a blind retrieve.) Then return with him to the line. Line your dog up facing in the direction of the dummies and say the cue "dead bird" again.

Send him for each dummy in turn, using the command "back" (or another you have chosen) and generously reinforcing each successful retrieve. (If the dog doesn't find the dummy, you may have gone out too far. Try again at a shorter distance.) You can gradually increase the distance of your sight blinds until your dog is performing reliably out to 100 yards or more. Also mix up dummies and birds from time to time to keep it interesting. Lining drills can be boring for both dog and handler.

Lining: The Traditional Approach ...

Most retriever trainers teach lining as described above—by working the dog in one area before moving to a new location. They believe that lining is a particularly challenging behavior to teach and prefer that it be solid in one place before introducing the distractions of a new environment. This is the standard approach to generalization.

... And an Alternative

Some positive trainers, however, do not hold the location constant while introducing lining drills, but vary it from the beginning so that the dog focuses on the target, not on the environment. We do not have any direct experience in using this approach to teach lining, but it may well work if you manage it carefully. The approach is to teach the dog to touch the target when the target is placed in several different locations, gradually increasing the distance and then decreasing the size of the target. The objective is to teach the dog to run out even if she does not actually see the target, in the hope that she will interpret the cue to mean that she should run out until halted, regardless of location. (We discuss halting the dog with a whistle signal later.)

A variation of sight blinds, used by some British trainers, is to set up a line of dummies along a wall or hedge and send the dog for each in turn. You walk out along the line with your dog and drop one dummy, saying "dead bird," at the far end. Then turn back with your dog and let him see you drop, and hear you verbally mark, several more dummies as you return to the sending line. Send your dog for the dummies, again reinforcing each successful retrieve. Once your dog is proficient at this, you can try stealthily dropping a dummy so that your dog doesn't see it. If you have built up good momentum and trust with your earlier drills, your dog probably will "take the line" to the unseen dummy, because he has learned that "back" means there is something exciting out there.

You can also train the dog to take a line by targeting. As described in Chapter 2, targeting trains a dog to touch an object on command. For a dog that is skilled at targeting, it's a relatively simple matter to go out to an object at increasingly greater distances. You can begin by having your dog target a flag in your hand, for example, and then one stuck in the ground. You can get small, highly visible flags from gun dog supply companies. Some people use a white bucket, but we will use "flag" here to mean any visible target for your dog. You can then move the flag out farther from the dog. This is where a "reward marker" is essential; if you can't deliver the primary reinforcer to the dog when he reaches the flag, you can mark it with a click or verbal marker, and deliver the primary reinforcer when you reach the dog.

When the dog is fluently targeting the flag, you can start to put dummies (or birds) at the base of the flag. If your dog is an enthusiastic retriever, he will find the opportunity to pick up and return the dummies reinforcing in itself, so you can click when he gets to the flag and the retrieve becomes the reinforcer. Use the "dead bird" cue before you send him. Keep moving the flag out until the dog is going consistently 100 yards or more.

When you reach this stage, it's time to begin to reduce the visibility of the flag and transition the dog to going out even if there is no prominent object to target. Place the flag in the ground near a tree, bush, rock, or something else visible in the yard. Send the dog to that spot for several training sessions. Then, one evening when your dog is sleeping at your feet, take a pair of scissors and cut about 20% of the flag off and throw it away. (This is why we really like the inexpensive flags!) Repeat the lining drill with the smaller flag for several days and then cut off another 20% or so. Repeat this until all that is left is the little wooden flagstaff. Then try getting rid of that as well. There's a good chance that the dog will have transferred the target to the tree, bush, or rock. As long as there's something there to retrieve, he'll probably keep going out.

Work diligently until you have reached the stage of fluency and then move on to generalization. Set up the "disappearing flag" drill in several new locations, some with less prominent natural features. Watch your dog's head carefully, and send him out only when he is looking in the right direction. This takes close observation and good timing. After a while your dog will learn something like, "Well, I'm not sure I see anything out there, but in the past whenever the boss sent me in the direction I was looking, there was a bird there. I think I'll run out there and see what happens!"

Another drill that many trainers use for lining is called "wagon wheel casting." Imagine that you and your dog are at the center of a wagon wheel and that there are several bumpers out along the spokes near the rim (see Figure 7.2). Start with four bumpers, positioned at 90-degree angles from each other. Line your dog up facing one and send him. When he returns, line him up for the next, and so on. Gradually increase the number of bumpers. Some pros go up to 16 bumpers or more and alternate close-in bumpers with others that are farther away. They also alternate white bumpers with orange ones, which are very difficult for dogs to see against a grassy background. If you and your dog enjoy this drill, it can reinforce good lining.

7.2 Wagon Wheel Casting

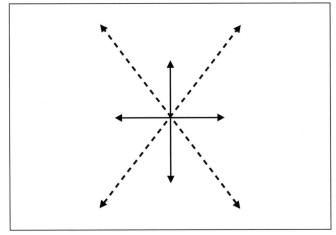

An eight-bumper wagon wheel: the solid arrows represent paths to white bumpers, the dashed arrows to orange ones. You can start with fewer bumpers and add more.

Sometimes you and your dog will be lucky. The blind will be on a straight line from you, the wind will be in your favor, the dog will be looking exactly the right way, and he will go directly to the bird, find it, and bring it back. But this does not happen often! It's more likely that the dog will stray from a direct line, or that there will be obstacles that prevent him from going straight to the bird. In that case, you will have to direct him. But first, you will have to get his attention.

Whistle Stop

To get the attention of a gun dog that is running out along a line, you need to get him to stop and look back at you. The way to do this most effectively is to train him to stop on a whistle command. The whistle sound will carry much farther than your voice will and—unlike your voice—it will not carry the emotional charge that you may feel if your dog is going the wrong way!

Most retriever trainers use a single blast on the whistle ("tweet") for a remote sit. (They use a trill, or series of blasts—"tweet, tweet, tweet"—for a recall.) It's easy to teach a dog to sit on a whistle. Simply blow the whistle, and then give the "sit" command, either by voice or hand signal, whichever is stronger for your dog. The sequence is important. The new cue (the whistle) must precede the known cue. If the new cue comes after the familiar cue it adds no new information and, since it has no meaning, the dog will probably ignore it. (This is called overshadowing and is explained in Chapter 1.) If the cues come at the same time, they can block each other and confuse the dog. So always use the new cue before the familiar one.

After a number of repetitions, which will vary depending on the dog, you can blow the whistle and wait for a couple of seconds. If the dog sits, you can then begin to use the whistle cue alternately with others that the dog knows. Continue to use the whistle frequently until you are confident that the dog knows this signals a sit. Then you can begin to incorporate having him turning around to face you.

There are several ways to do this. A good way to begin is to start with your dog standing or walking a short way from you. Call your dog using your recall command and, before he reaches you, blow the sit whistle. It may take several tries, but eventually the dog will sit facing you. C/T and repeat until he can do this reliably. (Remember also to give him plenty of recalls without the whistle sit; you want to keep his speed and enthusiasm up for returning with the bird and for coming when called in general.)

A variation on this approach is to blow the sit whistle when your dog is away from you, and if he does not face you when he sits, give the recall command. When he turns to come to you, give the sit whistle again. C/T when he is sitting facing you.

Finally, if your dog doesn't seem to be getting it, you can shape the behavior. (See Chapter 1 for an explanation of shaping by approximation.) After you are sure the whistle sit is solid, begin to reinforce your dog when he sits slightly turned to you, and withhold the reinforcer when he is facing directly away. Moving in small steps, you can gradually shape the dog to turn more and more toward you. Keep the rate of reinforcement high, and back up if it begins to slip. Always progress at the dog's pace. Eventually, this type of shaping can lead to a strong behavior.

The last step in training the whistle stop is to be sure that your dog is looking at you after he sits. With clicker training, this is a simple matter of watching the dog carefully and, the instant he looks at you, C/T. When he is looking at you after sitting reliably, you can require slightly longer periods of attention—five seconds is sufficient—before the C/T.

When the whistle stop is fluent in the yard at short distances, you can begin to generalize. Gradually increase the distance and level of distraction. Proof the behavior by requiring whistle sits for a variety of reinforcers—supper, happy bumpers, walks, and games. Add distance in low distraction areas, then reduce distance and add more distractions. Work carefully and patiently; it takes time to get a retriever to stop, sit, and watch at a distance when there are a lot of other interesting things around. Try to read your dog's behavior and move in slow steps. Don't, for example, try to get him to stop and look at you when he's chasing a squirrel or tracking an interesting scent without first ensuring that he's reliable in easier circumstances. It will save both you and your dog a lot of frustration.

One additional point. While we often mention 80% as a standard for increasing criteria on a behavior, we have a different standard for the whistle stop—100%! This is because you need a reliable way to interrupt unwanted behavior at a great distance and of course you are not using an electronic collar for that purpose. So you need a foolproof way to stop an unsuccessful trial and set up again. Only a completely solid whistle stop or recall will accomplish this.

Casting

Once your dog is reliably sitting at a distance on your whistle signal, you can begin to teach directional control, or "casting." A cast is a hand or voice signal that tells your dog to move out in a particular direction. The purpose of casting is to send your dog in a direction that will bring him to the area in which the bird has fallen. It may take several casts to do this, especially if there are obstacles or other factors to overcome.

There are two basic types of casts: "over" and "back." As the terms suggest, the over casts tell the dog to move to the side and the back casts tell him to turn around and move away from you. There are two variations of each type: the "right over," "left over," "right back," and "left back." The photographs in Figure 7.3 show the correct way to give casting signals. Because your dog will have to understand these signals when far away from you, it is important that they be precise and distinct. Remember that dogs have poorer visual acuity than we do, but have a superior ability to detect motion. So be sure to move your body in a way that is easy for your dog to see and, when you first begin to train casting, wear clothing that contrasts with the background. It's useful to practice your casting signals in front of a mirror. Face the mirror in your training clothes and do the following:

For the over casts: Turn your body to the right or left, extend your arm outward (right arm for right over, left arm for left over) parallel to the ground, and take a step over. You can use the word "over" before you step. (It's best to say the word prior to the motion, to prevent "blocking" the cue.)

For the back casts: Face the dog and extend your right or left arm straight up, while taking a step forward with the leg on the same side as the arm with which you are signaling. You can use the word "back" before you step. (This is the same word most US trainers use to send a dog on a blind, so if it seems to confuse your dog, select another cue.)

When your signals are clear and distinct, you can begin to teach your dog to respond to them. Below, we describe two methods for teaching casting. The first is a traditional method, used by retriever trainers for many years. The second is based on the "go out" command used by competitive obedience and agility trainers, and ultimately derived from the work that the Baileys did in training many species of animals to work at a distance. Currently, this is not typically used by retriever trainers, but it provides a viable alternative that you may want to investigate.

The first, traditional method is based on a technique used by British trainer Eric Begbie. British handlers place great emphasis on preparing their dogs with thorough obedience training. We agree. For this drill, it is very important that your dog have a reliable sit-stay and whistle stop. If he doesn't, work on these commands and wait until he is solid before you begin casting work.

Here's the way to start. You will need a couple of dummies and a whistle.

Sit your dog facing you about 5 yards away and tell him to stay. Throw one dummy about 10 yards to your left, wait 10 seconds, and throw the other dummy 10 yards to your right.

Wait another 10 seconds and then give the cast to send your dog to the left. If the dog moves in the correct direction, let him retrieve the dummy and return it to you; C/T. If he starts off in the wrong direction, give the sit signal with your whistle. Go out to your dog, heel him in the direction of the correct dummy, and send him to retrieve it from there. When he returns it to you, C/T. Repeat this drill for several days. After he is reliably retrieving the dummy to the left, spend several days sending him for a dummy to the right. Again, C/T him if he gets it right, but if he heads the wrong way, stop him with your whistle and when he is once more looking at you, resend him.

After about a week of retrieving one dummy, make it more complicated by sitting your dog and varying the order in which you send him in each direction. Occasionally send him for one dummy, make him sit, throw it again, and make him retrieve it a second time before sending him for the other dummy.

7.3 Casting Signals

Left back   *Right back*

Left over   *Right over*

When he can retrieve on a cast from either side, repeat the procedure but throw the dummies behind and slightly to the side of the dog instead of straight out to the right and left. Use the right or left back signals to send the dog. Be sure he turns in the correct direction. If he does not, stop him and redirect him, as you did with the over cast. Once again, spend several days on the right back, several on the left back, and then work with two dummies in the field.

Once your dog knows all four directions, you can proof the behavior in two ways. One way is to add distance by throwing the dummies farther away.

If you have a dummy launcher, you can use it to extend the distance even farther. Then, you can make the task more complex by throwing three dummies, and later throwing a dummy in each of the four directions.

Retriever trainers have different opinions about whether you should start with over casts or back casts, and whether you should start with one dummy before you add a second thrown in a different direction, or start with two. We have seen all of these approaches work. If you are concerned that your dog may be confused by a second dummy, by all means work on each direction for a few days with only one before adding the second. And if your dog doesn't seem to be getting the over cast, drop it and try the backs. Finally, if your dog doesn't seem to be getting it at all, you can shape the turns by reinforcing any move in the correct direction and gradually requiring more movement toward the dummy.

The other way to proof the behavior is based on Morgan Spector's technique for teaching "go out." In advanced obedience training, a go out requires that the dog go 30 feet away from the handler, stop, turn, and sit on command.

To train this behavior, Spector uses a target stick. (See Chapter 2 for the basics of training targeting.) He plants one end of the target stick in the ground a distance away from the dog. He then sends the dog to the stick using the targeting command, for example "touch," and delivers a C/T for each successful performance. He keeps the distance short enough to maintain a high rate of reinforcement. Gradually he extends the distance.

To use this technique for casting, begin with the dog sitting facing you and the target stick to the dog's right (your left). Give your hand and voice signal for the cast, and then give the targeting command. Extend distance as Spector describes. When the behavior is solid, begin to fade the targeting command and use the casting commands only. Repeat for each of the four directions. Raise the criteria gradually for distance, speed, and running straight to the target, always striving to keep a high rate of reinforcement. When the dog will go to the target stick at some 20 yards in each direction, you can begin to place a dummy there. If the dog picks it up naturally, the retrieve can become the reinforcer. If not, you may have to use the command "fetch." Once the dog consistently picks up dummies on each casting signal, you can begin to fade the presence of the target stick. (You can use a collapsible pointer, so that you can make it smaller and gradually eliminate it altogether.)

We haven't used this method, but some of our colleagues have, to good effect. If you do try this method, please report the results to us.

Proofing Your Casts: Two Baseball Games

We recommend two drills to keep your dog's casting sharp.

An Experimental Technique

Some positive trainers have begun to use a remote treat delivery device called Treat & Train to teach directional control. (For more information, see Chapter 2.)

You can use the stationary baseball drill after your dog knows all of the casts. You will need quite a few bumpers. To begin, imagine that you and your pup are on a baseball diamond, as in Figure 7.4. Sit the dog at the pitcher's mound, facing home plate. Toss several bumpers each to first, second, and third base. Then walk to home plate and stand facing the dog. (See Figure 7.4.)

Pick one of the bases and cast your dog toward it. When he retrieves the dummy, walk out to meet him at the mound, turn so he will face home plate when he comes to heel, and take the dummy when he delivers. C/T. Heel him back to the mound and place him in a sit-stay. Return to home, turn, and send him for another dummy. Alternate directions, ensuring that your dog turns the proper way toward second base when you give the right and left back casts.

7.4 Stationary Baseball

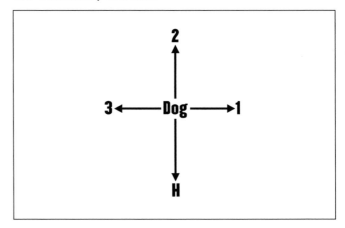

Stationary baseball can get boring after a while, so you can add enthusiasm for casting with a drill called "walking baseball" (see Figure 7.5). To do this drill, you don't need a baseball diamond—just find a good area in your yard where you can be a distance away from the dog. You will need two bumpers. Start with the dog sitting in front of you about 10 yards away. Throw a bumper in one direction, say to the left. Then walk away from the dog in a direction other than the one in which you threw the bumper. Stop about 20 yards from your dog, face him, and throw the second bumper in another direction, for example to the right. Now cast him to the first bumper you threw.

7.5 Walking Baseball

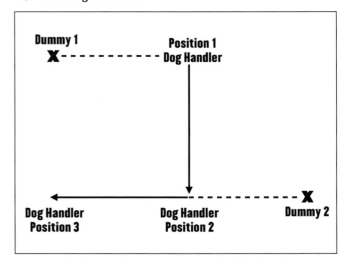

When your dog returns with the first bumper, take it and walk about 20 yards in another direction, keeping him in a sit-stay. When you get to your new position, toss the bumper you just took away from him. Send him for the second bumper you tossed. (We know this can be a little confusing; look at the diagram or, better yet, try it in the yard and it will become clearer.) Take the second dummy from him, walk away, toss the bumper away, and send him for the previous bumper. You can keep this up for a number of repetitions, varying the distance between you and your dog and the directions of the casts. We also like to occasionally leave the dog in a stand-stay and have him do a whistle sit before casting.

You will find lively and sometimes emotional debates among retriever trainers about matters such as whether walking baseball should precede or follow pattern blinds (discussed later in this chapter). We have seen gun dogs trained successfully both ways. We suggest that you look at the professional retriever trainers' books and videos, pick a sequence that makes sense to you, and stick with it, substituting positive reinforcement for the correction-based methods.

Putting It Together

Now your dog can take a line, stop on a whistle, and obey directional signals. It's time to go out into the field and run blinds, right? Wrong! We need to put the pieces together into the "chain" that your dog must perform when doing a blind retrieve. The way to do this is through a series of exercises called T-drills. This name is used because the exercises all use patterns based on the letter T. There are three types: "mini-T," "single-T," and "double-T." The descriptions that follow are based on Mike Lardy's training method, minus the "force." (For details, see Lardy's article, "Double T," in *The Retriever Journal*, December/January 1996–97, pp. 33–35.)

These are challenging drills, for both you and your dog. So be sure to use appropriate reinforcers to celebrate successes, and take a break and simplify if your progress wanes.

Proofing Casts: The Traditional Approach ...

Professional retriever trainers who rely on electronic collars use a technique called "indirect pressure" during casting exercises. When a dog makes a mistake (and especially if it appears to be from lack of effort rather than confusion), the handler commands "sit" with the whistle, and then delivers a stimulus from the electronic collar. The intensity and duration of the stimulus depends, in these trainers' view, on the severity of the dog's infraction. The idea is that the dog will associate the unpleasant stimulus with the error and will be less likely to repeat it.

... And an Alternative

Our assumption is that dogs rarely make mistakes out of laziness or lack of effort. They may appear to do so, but Morgan's Canon of Parsimony requires us to look for explanations that involve lower-level processes. From this perspective, failures are more likely to stem from confusion, distraction, or boredom. The step-by-step drills necessary to teach blind retrieves can be repetitive and boring for both dog and handler, and we think it is inappropriate to punish dogs when they don't perform these exercises as well as we would like. In addition, we find the idea of punishing a dog when she did what we asked (the sit) to be inconsistent with our understanding of learning theory. Instead, we prefer to increase the value of the reinforcers (better treats or happy bumpers) and to analyze the situation to see what might be confusing or distracting for the dog. We also find that walking baseball, covered in this chapter, can improve the dog's responsiveness.

7.6 Double-T Drill

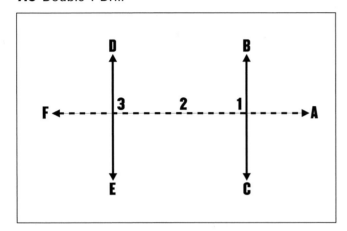

To begin, you will need a lot of bumpers. You will also need a lot of space; Lardy recommends a field at least 100 yards long and 50 yards wide. Start by setting up five piles of several bumpers each, in the locations labeled "A through E" in Figure 7.6. There is one center pile at A and four side piles at B, C, D, and E. Each side pile is about 20 yards from the center line. The distant side piles (B and C) are 25 yards in from the center pile; the nearer side piles (D and E) are 25 yards out from the baseline (F).

To start your training, walk your dog out to a line about 15 yards from the distant center pile (A) and let him watch as you toss another bumper. Then send your dog to the pile, either from your side, or from a position facing you about five yards out. While your dog is running to the pile, back up 10 to 15 yards, and receive the bumper when the dog delivers it. Set your dog up and send him to the pile from this new position. Once again, move back 10 to 15 yards, and receive the bumper. Continue this process—send, back up, receive—until you have reached the baseline (F) of your double-T, about 100 yards from the distant center pile. Send the dog from the baseline to the pile several times—a couple from your side and a couple from a remote sit—and call it a day. (If your dog veers from the center line toward the side piles, stop him with the whistle and set up again; if he does this consistently, shorten the distance and work back more gradually.)

On your next training day, start the process again by tossing a bumper to the distant pile, but back up more quickly toward the baseline. Your goal is to

have the dog reliably running to the most distant pile (the "back" pile) from either side of the remote position. If necessary, shorten the distance and move back more slowly until he masters the process.

The next step is to stop your dog when he is on the way to the pile. Warm your dog up by having him do several whistle sits, then bring him to the line and have him sit in the heel position. Send your dog from the baseline and, when he is running for the back pile, stop him with your whistle. Then send him with a "back" cast to the pile. When he returns, send him again, but this time without the whistle stop. Dogs that are stopped too often during this drill may develop the habit of "popping," which is a tendency to stop and look back for direction, rather than running quickly to the pile. Keep the ratio of whistle stops to direct returns fairly low— no more than one out of three retrieves—to minimize the chance of popping. While doing this drill, you can also reinforce your dog's whistle stop by stopping him occasionally when he is returning with the bumper, and then giving the "come" whistle for him to resume.

Next you can work on the mini-T. Walk out with your dog to the intersection of the more distant "T" (point 1 in Figure 7.6). Toss a couple of bumpers to each of the side piles (B and C). Sit your dog facing you and cast him alternately to each of the side piles, occasionally mixing in a cast to the back pile (A).

Once the casting is solid, back up to a point halfway between the sets of side piles (point 2 in Figure 7.6). Send your dog from that point toward the back pile when he reaches the intersection (point 1); stop him with your whistle. Now cast him to one of the three piles. Repeat, mixing up the piles. If your dog heads in the wrong direction, stop him and cast him in the correct path. If he consistently goes the wrong way, back up, simplify, and work up to the mini-T later.

When your dog is proficient with the mini-T, you can convert it to a full-T by backing up and sending your dog from the baseline. You will probably need several days of full-T work. If your dog heads for one of the side piles instead of for the distant center pile, you may need to shorten the distance and move back gradually until he is clear about the concept of running straight until stopped.

When you have mastered the full-T, you and your dog are ready to try the demanding double-T drill. Begin by repeating the process that you used when teaching your dog the two side piles, but this time with the nearer piles (D and E in Figure 7.6). Sit him between the piles and cast alternately to the right and left. Then back up to the baseline and send him for the pile at A. Stop him either at the point of the nearer piles (3) or the farther ones (1) and cast him to either side. Again, alternate whistle sits and casts with direct retrieves to minimize popping.

Pattern Blinds

You will soon be able to test your dog's abilities with simple blind retrieves. But first, you need to get him used to running out a considerable distance when he hasn't seen anything fall. You can begin this process with "pattern blinds." For this exercise, you will need a lot of dummies and a big yard, preferably one at least 100 yards square. If you don't have one, try a ball field or public park, if you can run your dog off-lead or on a check cord safely. At this stage of training, however, try to keep the dog in a mowed area or one with very low cover. You will have plenty of time to introduce higher cover, more difficult terrain, and other distractions—what retriever trainers call "factors"—later in your training program.

To begin training pattern blinds, go to the yard without your dog and set up a pile of dummies at the opposite end from your sending line, at a distance that you believe will be comfortable for your dog. Then bring your dog out, set him up facing the pile, and give the "dead bird" cue. When your dog is looking squarely in the direction of the pile, send him with a "back." Do this for several days; you can gradually extend the distance, as long as the dog is successful consistently. Remember to provide a high rate of reinforcement, as you do when training any new behavior.

When your dog has mastered retrieving from the pile, repeat the process, but this time with the pile in a new location. Ideally, it should be at about the same distance you started from with the first pile but in a different direction from the sending line, preferably about 90 degrees to the right or left. Then repeat the process you used with the first pile, again maintaining a high ROR.

The next step is to repeat the drill with a third pile, 90 degrees in the opposite direction from the second pile.

When your dog has finished these drills, he will have mastered three different blind patterns. You can then set up two piles at a time and send him for one or two retrieves from each pile. If you are careful about watching the direction of his gaze, he will go to the correct one. You can use your hand to signal when to go, but realize that dogs don't naturally use pointing with their paws to indicate direction, so they won't necessarily understand where you are pointing unless you have trained the "go out." You may, as one researcher did, have better luck if you put a paper cone on your nose to simulate a dog's snout and use it to point toward the pile. But you'd look pretty silly wearing one at a hunt test!

Finally, you can begin to send your dog alternately to each of the three piles. You can also extend the direction and narrow the angle, by moving your sending line back. The last step is to add "diversions." These are distractions such as people, decoys, and other objects. You can also have your dog retrieve a thrown bird and then follow up with a pattern blind. As long as you can keep the ROR high, your dog will learn successfully.

When working on blinds, it's useful to remember external inhibition (Chapter 1). Expect occasional lapses, be patient, and take breaks when learning seems to be flagging. It will almost certainly return.

Cold Blinds

At last, the big day has come. You are ready to start running "cold blinds," which are blind retrieves in areas that are new to the dog. Pick a fairly level field with low cover and avoid days when the wind is heavy. Go out before your dog and set up several blinds spread out at wide angles in the field, about 100 yards from the line. Mark them with orange tape or poles; you will be able to see them distinctly but your dog won't. (Orange, green, and brown all look about the same to dogs.) Try to set the blinds in places where your dog will be able to see them easily once he gets near and, if possible, set them upwind or crosswind from the sending line.

Then bring your dog out. Sit him in the heel position, facing one of the blinds. Use your "dead bird" cue or whatever signal you are using to indicate a blind. When he is looking at the area of the blind, send him on the command "back." If you've done your homework, he should head out in the general direction of the bird or dummy.

If you are really lucky, your dog will head directly for the blind, pick it up, and return. But it's much more likely that he will drift off the line. If so, stop him with your whistle, and cast him in the proper direction. Once he gets the dummy and returns it to you, C/T generously. Then send him for one of the other blinds. Stick with two or three repetitions each day, and keep the setups simple. His confidence and performance will improve with each success.

Water Handling

So far, we've been working on casts exclusively on land. Teaching a dog to take casts in the water is similar to the process we use on land. Make sure that the dog is fluent in casting on land and that you have generalized that behavior to include different distances and different terrain. In addition, of course, you will need some water. The ideal setup is a rectangular or oval pond of swimming depth about 15 yards wide and 30 yards long (see Figure 7.7). You can train in this pond by setting up a water variation of the T-drills described above.

7.7 Water-T

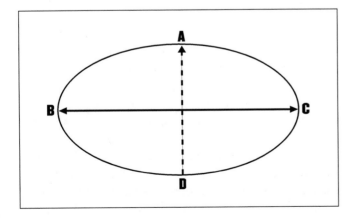

Start by dropping a pile of dummies straight across the width of the pond from your sending line (to point A in Figure 7.7). Let the dog see them. Then take him to the line and toss another dummy across the pond, into the pile. Send him from point D across the pond to the dummies several times until it's clear he knows where the pile is and is swimming for it energetically. Then, when he's about halfway across, blow your stop whistle. At first, he'll probably think you are nuts; there's nothing to sit on! You may have to whistle again, call him by name, or give a recall command for him to realize he's supposed to turn around and tread water. You may even have to stop him by pulling gently on a check cord, but that's a last resort. Once he stops, use your back cast to send him to the pile. Keep it up until he stops and treads water and then takes a back cast reliably. Be sure to mix direct retrieves from the pile with stops, so that he continues to head into the water with confidence.

At this point, you can proceed as you did with the land T-drill. Set piles at the ends of the pond (points B and C), and stop your dog and then cast him to each of them. Again, be sure to include plenty of retrieves from directly across the pond. Then intermix over and back casts until your dog is responding well to all of them.

Swim-By

There is another drill that professional retrievers use for water work, the often misunderstood "swim-by." Swim-by gets its name because the dog is required to swim by you, with a bumper in his mouth. The point of this drill is to teach the dog that he must continue swimming in the direction he is sent until he receives another command, rather than automatically exiting the water to return to you. In addition to improving his handling in the water, the swim-by will teach your dog to remain in the water until called, reducing the likelihood that he will "cheat" by returning to land early on water retrieves. (While this may not be a big deal to you in a hunting situation, cheating on a water retrieve is a cardinal sin in hunt tests and field trials.)

Swim-by is an elaborate process that we will not cover in this book. An excellent description appears in an article by professional trainer Evan Graham in *Retriever Journal*, April/May 2004.

Water Blinds (Channel Blinds)

"Channel blinds" are a good way to introduce your dog to the challenge of blind retrieves in the water. Find a body of water that is narrower than it is long, such that it forms a channel. It doesn't need to be very long; 25 to 30 yards should be enough. Also, it's useful to train the channel blind in a place where the dog has previously done water marks.

Set up a short blind on the water and send your dog from the line down the channel (see Figure 7.8). If he deviates from the line, stop him with your whistle and cast him in the proper direction. If he exits the water before completing the retrieve, he may be confused or uncomfortable. Meet him quietly so you don't reinforce the error, simplify the task, and try again. Once he is confidently lining and taking your casts, you can extend the distance again. The idea is to keep the dog swimming as directly as possible toward the blind and back. If he exits onto the land, you can withhold the C/T or, if the behavior is persistent, use the negative punishment of a brief time-out. By combining patient, systematic training with great reinforcers, you should be able to teach your dog the channel blind.

7.8 Channel Blind

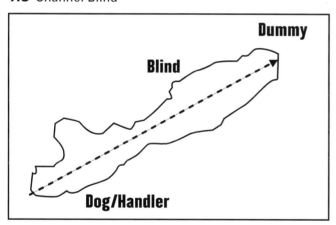

After you have run channel blinds of varying distances for a while, you can try a blind that requires a water exit and reentry if you have a suitable training area. You can also incorporate diversions, such as running a short mark before the channel blind, to proof your dog's performance (see Figure 7.9).

7.9 Reentry with Diversion

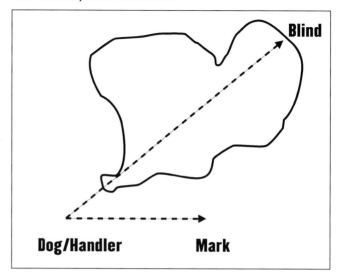

At this point, you are ready to try some cold water blinds. ("Cold" refers to blinds in new places, not to the temperature of the water.) Go to a new body of water. Keep the setups simple at first. Send your dog to the area of the blind, casting as necessary to keep him on line. You can gradually increase distance and complexity and, eventually, combine land and water blinds. You can do this by having the dog run a distance on land before entering the water or by planting the blind on land a distance from the opposite shore. Eventually, your dog will learn to do multiple water entries and exits and to cope with other complicating factors.

Don't Fear the Factors: Advanced Training and Generalization

Retriever trainers identify a number of factors that affect the difficulty of a retrieve. They include: wind speed and direction; water depth, current, and temperature; number of water entries and exits; height and heaviness of cover; and changes in terrain such as hills, ditches, and walls. All of these complicate the retrieving task, and your dog must be "proofed" against them. This is the generalization stage of training, and it's essential to work diligently so that you can reach "maintenance" and then take your dog hunting or testing with confidence.

If possible, isolate these factors, and train your dog to handle each of them, one at a time. The chance of isolating factors is rare, however, since the land, water, and weather are unlikely to adhere to your training schedule. Yet you can monitor these factors and try to progress at a pace that will permit your dog to succeed. For instance, if you are working on terrain and haven't yet started working with high winds, you have two options. The first is to take your dog out on a non-windy day. The second is, assuming you have worked the terrain to a specific level of proficiency, to take the dog out and work in the wind while working a much lower level of terrain difficulty than you would on a non-windy day. As always, the rule is to maintain a high rate of reinforcement, whether your reinforcer is praise, treats, or a happy bumper. If the ROR starts to slip, simplify, simplify, simplify!

Decheating: The Traditional Approach ...

Decheating is training the dog not to "cheat" or deviate from a straight line on the way to or back from a blind. The common way of dealing with cheating is to use electronic collar corrections when the dog deviates from a straight line. After a number of repetitions, the dog learns to avoid the shock by coming directly back to the handler.

... And an Alternative

Another, albeit largely untested, method of decheating is to use an intermediate bridge or keep-going signal (KGS). You begin by conditioning the KGS by sounding it, followed by a click or other reward marker (see Chapter 4 for detailed instructions). The dog learns that when he hears the KGS, he is on the correct path to a reinforcement.

To use this on a blind is difficult, but can be done with the praise tone on some electronic collars. By hearing the sound of the tone continuously as he maintains a straight line, the dog learns that if he keeps going, the reinforcer—retrieve or treat—will come next!

Professional trainers' programs have a number of excellent advanced drills that can help you with proofing. We suggest that you run as many of these drills as possible, substituting positive reinforcement for the "force" aspects.

It is also useful to train with a gun dog club if there is one in your area. The national breed clubs maintain lists of local clubs. Many local breed clubs have formal training programs or informal training days. Some are led by professional trainers. You will find other sporting breed enthusiasts there and perhaps be able to see how different breeds work. It's a great kick to see hard-driving Labs, enthusiastic tollers, and elegant standard poodles retrieve.

As a positive trainer, you may be in the minority at these events and will have to explain what that little plastic box next to the whistle and duck call on your lanyard is. You may encounter some skepticism or even hostility. And you may see treatment of dogs that, by our standards, borders on being abusive. But you and your dog will get experience in working around other dogs, people, and distractions. You will also get valuable insights about how experienced trainers deal with the factors and probably some good advice about how to introduce them to your dog. You probably will be counseled to force fetch your dog or get an electronic collar. Our suggestion is to acknowledge the advice, then set these proposals aside, focus on the training tasks rather than the method, and use the sessions to proof your dog for new situations.

You're On Your Way!

If you've been diligent about your training, you are well on your way to having a reliable hunting retriever. You should be able to take him with confidence on a short hunt and to run hunt tests up to the Senior Hunter level. There will always be more to train and more to learn, but you can take pride in your dog's accomplishments and enjoy watching him do the work that he was born to do.

Chapter 8

Upland Hunting

Find It, Point It, Flush It, and Get It!

Retrieving is a skill common to most gun dog breeds, but after that they diverge. Many retrievers do their work from a duck blind or boat, where their handlers call the ducks in. Retriever tests and trials follow this pattern. But other gun dogs, and some retrievers as well, work in the uplands—hunting, pointing, and flushing birds in addition to retrieving.

There are two primary styles of upland hunting over dogs. Spaniels and other flushing dogs hunt by working an area within shooting range of the hunter, flushing up the bird so the hunter has a good shot. In this style of hunting, the dog and hunter work closely as a team. This means that the hunter needs to pay close attention and read his dog's body language or he may miss the shot that is flushed up in front of him or somewhere off to the side.

8.1 Hardy

Champion Hillcrest Just Hale N Hardy VCD1, OA, SH, WDX, CDX, RE, a spaniel with obedience, rally, agility, and field titles. (Photograph by owner and handler Farr Hinton; used with permission.)

Hunting with pointing and setting breeds is a cooperative effort, but each team member (dog and hunter) takes a turn in his or her part of the game. Pointing and setting breeds are bred to range far from the hunter, locate a bird, get as close as possible to it without making it flush, point it out, and wait for the hunter to get there to flush it up. (In some European countries, however, the pointing dog can flush the bird on command.) Generally this makes for easier shots for the hunter because he knows better where and when the bird is going to get up, with fewer surprises.

Whether you hunt with a flusher or a pointer or setter is usually a style preference; however, the timing within the season can make a difference. In the beginning of the season when the birds usually sit tighter for longer, hunting with a pointer or setter can be great fun. However, it's more frustrating at the end of the season when many of the birds turn into runners, which makes pointing a difficult task. The relationship is different, and the hunting style is different, but clearly there is overlap in the skills the dogs must have. One thing is certain: whatever your preference among the types of gun dogs, there is nothing more beautiful and gratifying than watching your dogs working a section of field, seeing a flusher work a hot spot until the bird gets up, or seeing a pointer or setter in full body intensity while on point!

Gun Conditioning

Before you can hunt over your dog, you have to ensure that she is not gun-shy. Some dogs naturally seem fine with the sound of gunfire and are never fazed by it. Some are a bit gun-shy, but the thrill of the hunt is greater than their fear of the gunfire sound and they'll hunt enthusiastically anyway. Then there are those that are so startled by, and afraid of, the sound of gunfire that they hightail it back to you or the vehicle and become a quivering mass, unable to hunt at all.

The old wives' tale of gun conditioning is that you should just fire gunshots over your dog's head while she is eating. This may work sometimes; however, without proper conditioning, you may end up with a dog that is afraid of a bizarre list of things in addition to the gunfire, such as the type of surface she was standing on at the time, the food she was eating or the food dish she was eating from, the kind of shoes you were wearing when you fired the shot, the ant she happened to notice walk by at the time of the shot, and so on.

In order to maximize your chance of having a dog that is comfortable with the sound of gunfire and minimize the risk of developing fears of strange things, we recommend that you take her through a process called "gun conditioning," or desensitizing her to the sound of gunfire through systematic classical conditioning.

When you first get your puppy or adopt an older dog, start to accustom her to loud noises around the house before you consider introducing gunfire. These noises can include actions such as clapping hands, hitting a spoon on a pan, dropping a book, or slamming a door. When you first introduce the noises, choose a low-intensity noise first; for example, start with handclapping rather than slapping two pieces of wood together because the handclapping has a lower intensity sound. The goal is not to startle your dog, but to set her up to be successful. At a minimum, introduce the noise from across the room or, better yet, from another room in your house. It is helpful if you have a partner who can feed or play with your dog as the noise occurs and can tell you what her reaction is. If your dog is completely comfortable and doesn't react to the noise, then close your distance by a couple of feet and try again. As long as your dog is successful, you can continue to decrease the distance between you. Be patient with this process. If she ever appears startled or looks distressed by the noise, you are too close and need to back up several steps in the process (one or two steps earlier than your last success) and begin again, being careful not to forge ahead

too quickly. Gradually move on to higher intensity noises as you and your dog are successful. For some dogs this process will move along quickly, and for others it will take more time.

After experimenting with a variety of noises around the house, take your dog outside or to a field and introduce some of those same noises in that environment. Then add the sound of a cap gun or a starter pistol (using blanks, of course) at a long distance—approximately 50 yards—preferably while she is running and having fun, and ideally with another dog that is gunfire savvy. You can even walk around the area during this time, simulating the act of hunting. The process here is the same as before: close the distance gradually between you and your dog while she is having fun. Don't push this too quickly. Since dogs learn best when we practice in short, frequent intervals, only do about a dozen shots a day. If your dog reacts fearfully at any point, do not attempt to comfort her. Instead, pretend like nothing happened, and act interested in something else. When your dog reacts with fear, you again know that you have moved too close too quickly and need to take a few steps back in your conditioning.

When you are able to fire the cap gun at close range and your dog doesn't show any reaction to or interest in the sound, start the process over, this time with your shotgun. Again, feel free to simulate the hunting experience by strolling through the field with your dog and practicing other obedience skills as well. Bring along something you can use to muffle the sound of your shotgun if you need to. In addition to being mindful of the distance between you and your dog, you can also vary the conditions when you fire the gun; for example, sometimes fire when she is flushing a flock of birds, sometimes when she is in an all-out gallop, sometimes while she is intently sniffing the ground. The intent is to prevent the sound of gunfire from becoming a predictor of anything in particular at this point. You can train for that later in the process. For now, the gunfire noise should be just a part of the field experience.

By this time you should have a dog that is comfortable with the sound of gunfire and will be a great companion in the field. If your dog has serious gun-shyness problems, introducing this program at an extremely slow pace will help. For some dogs, it may be useful to introduce the gun while they are busy in a field of planted birds; the excitement that they feel may help them to overcome any anxiety about the noise. There are a couple of resources that can also help cure severe gun-shyness. Steve Rafe has an excellent system called Starfire Noiseshyness Cure Systems, and a company called Legacy by Mail also has a CD of the gunshot noise to help start this process at a very low intensity level. (See Appendix I for more information about these resources.)

Conditioning Is Critical!

While there is some question as to what the exact time periods are, it is generally accepted that dogs experience what are called "critical learning periods" between the ages of approximately 11 to 13 weeks, 5½ to 6½ months, 11 to 13 months, and 22 to 26 months. During these periods, a dog's responses to new experiences can be unpredictable, so be especially careful about introducing new noises and experiences, and make them as positive as possible for your dog at these ages.

Some Notes of Caution

The next skills that we describe are challenging for both handler and dog—and you will be working on them in highly distracting places. So here are some things to bear in mind as you set up your training program.

Do not try to train these field skills until your basic obedience is absolutely solid. In particular, you need a highly reliable whistle stop and recall (see Chapters 4 and 7) before you let your dog work off-lead in the field.

During initial training of any new skill, put a check cord on your dog to ensure that he doesn't get away from you and have a fun time doing something you don't want him to learn. Phase the check cord out

of the skills your dog knows well, and as he masters each new skill.

Also, remember that training sessions should be short but frequent rather than an hour-long marathon! Short sessions of five to ten minutes each are best.

Remember that as you build on these exercises, it's important to increase only one criterion at a time— just distance, just duration, or just the distraction level. For example, don't go from five steps distance and five seconds duration to ten steps distance and ten seconds duration during the initial learning process. You will do that later as a way to be unpredictable when the behavior is well ingrained, but in the learning stages it is important that you only work on one criterion at a time.

For pointing and flushing skills, criteria setting and record keeping are just as important as for any other training task. Keep note of your dog's progress, and any time that you fall below 50% success in a set of trials, or your dog fails in a task three times in a row, stop, take stock, go back, and try an easier approach.

Another key is not to move too fast. We often see people in classes saying their cues over and over again, bent over, holding their hand out, and engaging in an odd sort of moon walk in order to help keep their dogs in position. Those are their instincts telling them that they are moving too quickly! You should be able to use the verbal cue once, do what you planned to do in normal, relaxed human body posture, return to your dog, and release her without doing anything else physical to help her remain in place.

Quartering

Quartering is the primary skill that flushers and pointers and setters have in common. Quartering is essentially the way a dog works back and forth across the ground in front of the hunter in order to find birds, covering the ground as efficiently and effectively as possible. As we stated earlier, flushers tend to work ground that is closer to the hunter, while pointers and setters tend to roam farther and move faster in their ground work.

Reinforcement at a Distance...

One of the challenges of training pointing and flushing dogs (as well as retrievers) is the difficulty of reinforcing desired behavior when the dog is far away. There are several approaches to resolving this problem:

Recognize that some of the behaviors you are trying to train are part of the dog's predatory cycle and therefore are inherently reinforcing. Thus, you can click a dog for stopping on command and let the flush be the reinforcer. If you condition your dog that the clicker predicts a variety of reinforcers, including permission to engage in mock predatory behaviors, you can use clickers as reinforcers in the field.

You can also condition a keep-going signal or intermediate bridge, as described in Chapter 4. This tells the dog that he is on the right track and that the reinforcer will come in due course. You can use a voice or whistle signal or the praise tone on a remote collar. Kathy Sdao, a canine and marine mammal trainer from Washington State, reminded us that in a behavior chain like hunting, pointing, flushing, and retrieving, each behavior serves as a cue for the next, and therefore is a cue or keep-going signal in its own right. (Think of dogs running an agility course!) If we train that chain systematically, reinforcement occurs throughout the behavior sequence.

Finally, if you want to experiment, you can try the Treat & Train remote treat delivery system, which we've mentioned previously. Several retriever trainers we know are using it to good effect.

Step 1: For quartering, as for all gun dog skills, you need to split the skills rather than lumping them all together as one. That means that you start small and build gradually as your dog learns, starts to acquire, and then becomes fluent in the behaviors.

So with this step we start small and begin by making numerous back and forth direction changes with your dog while you are on your normal walks. Say "whoop!" or give a distinct double-peep on your whistle as a cue immediately preceding each time you make a direction change. Click and treat your dog for a successful turn. Start with a C/T for each turn (a continuous reinforcement schedule), and then reinforce less frequently (a variable reinforcement schedule), eventually eliminating the rewards for turns so that finding the dummy or bird becomes the final reward.

...But No "Correction"

What about "correcting" the dog's behavior if she does the wrong thing when she's far away? First, we recommend that you stop using the word "correction," which is a euphemism for punishment. As we have discussed throughout this book, we see no need for punishment if behaviors are trained step-by-step using positive methods. Of course dogs make mistakes (as do we), but such instances are usually either one-time errors or manifestations of an underlying training deficiency. We prefer to use our whistle stop or recall to interrupt the behavior and set up the drill again. If necessary, we will simplify the task. As a last resort, we may use negative punishment (for both the dogs and ourselves) and stop training for a time, or even head off for home. We often find that, in the next session, latent learning has taken over and the problem has disappeared.

Step 2: When direction changes start to become second nature to your dog, move to an area such as a softball field with short grass, and walk back and forth across the infield, moving slightly forward with each direction change as if you were "quartering" the field. Continue with your cue as in Step 1 prior to each direction change. Ideally you should start on the downwind side of the field and work back and forth into the wind since this is the preferred direction of the hunt (see Figure 8.2).

The width of your back-and-forth range should be relatively small to begin with so that you have more direction change repetitions; you can increase the width of the range as your dog understands what you are doing. The goal is for your dog to make the direction change on her own at the sound of your cue, all while working on a loose lead. Working on the end of a tight lead, or on a check cord as you add distance from your dog, will make it more difficult to transition to off-lead later.

8.2 Quartering Pattern

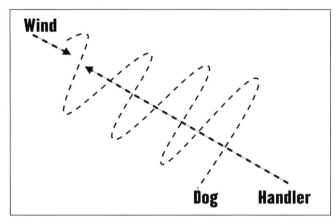

Step 3: Repeat Step 2, but start giving your dog more leash so she is directly out in front of you or to your forward side while you are "hunting" in an upwind direction in the softball field. Keep adding on leash distance until you are working with your dog as far ahead of you as you would like her to work. When you send your dog off to work the field, start adding your cue to release her to hunt. It can be "find the bird!" or "hunt it up!" or whatever you want to use. Over time, walk back and forth with your dog less and less, moving more in a straight ahead direction while your dog continues to work the field in a back-and-forth motion.

Step 4: Move your practice to an area with longer grass, or varying heights of grass, and repeat the skill as above. (You may have to return to Step 2, or even Step 1, when you do this.) Recognize that the distractions will be different, and there will be a wider variety of smells, so you will most likely have to work short distances with many direction changes when you move to this type of field. In this environment it may be helpful to use a nylon or plastic, braided rope to use as your check cord

because it will be less likely to get caught up in the grass or to tie itself up in knots.

Once your dog is solid on "whoa" work for pointers and setters (explained later in this chapter), or solid on sit to flush for flushers, start planting scented dummies in the field so he is able to find "birds" during his quartering sessions. Then progress to working with frozen, then thawed, then live birds in the field.

If you have an assistant, you can make directional changes more fluent by doing the following:

- Each person holds a bird or toy that the dog is interested in.

- The two people walk forward, staying abreast of each other (begin with only a few feet between you, and gradually increase the distance as the dog begins responding to the cue).

- Person A gives the cue (two whistle blasts) and person B begins waving the bird or toy to attract the dog's attention.

- Once the dog goes to person B, person A gives the cue and begins waving the bird or toy while person B hides his toy.

- Continue doing this until the dog responds to the cue without seeing the bird or toy and then begin gradually increasing the distance between handlers.

If three people are available, all three walk side-by-side, with the handler in the middle. The handler gives the cues and the two assistants handle the bird or toy. This technique allows the handler to cue the dog from any location.

If you are experiencing difficulty in getting the dog out to a reasonable distance, try laying a trail of dummies in a zigzag pattern that you can direct the dog on to as you walk forward up the center line of the trail. This method was suggested by British trainer Eric Begbie. Before you do this exercise, the dog needs to know lining and casting, as described in Chapter 7.

To start, establish that center line, either using existing landmarks or by placing a couple of pegs at either extreme. Make your center line 400 yards long. Then walk up the center line about 30 yards and place a dummy 15 yards out to the left. Then walk another 30 yards up the center line and place a dummy 15 yards out to the right. Then place another to the left and another to the right and so on until you have covered the distance of the center line.

Then get the dog. As you slowly walk up the center line, direct the dog to each dummy in turn in what will be, essentially, a series of blind retrieves.

Next time you do the exercise, skip some of the dummies, but still direct the dog out to where each would have been. That way he will become accustomed to moving to left and to right without always finding a dummy before being sent in the opposite direction.

An alternative, suggested by Irish gun dog trainer Des O'Neill, is the "cheese trick." Instead of laying out dummies, place pieces of cheese a few yards apart, in a zigzag pattern. Direct the dog back and forth (we would add a "click" just before he gets to the cheese). Over time, you can extend the distance, and then begin to skip some of the cheese bits. Eventually, a bird planted at the end of the pattern will provide motivation.

Pointing/Whoa

"Whoa" cues the dog to stop on command. Most pointers and setters will point naturally on birds due to their instincts, so many enthusiasts claim that teaching them the "whoa" command is an enormous waste of time. However, steadiness to wing and shot is important for the dog's safety if you have a low-flying bird and is one of the skills your dog will be scored on if you participate in hunt tests and field trials. A successful, solid whoa will provide the foundation for steadiness to wing and shot.

The whoa behavior is a staple of pointing and setting breeds. As in any behavior, in order to get predictable compliance you need to start small and gradually build on the skill by adding difficulty in the form of distance, duration of the behavior, distraction, and the environmental variables of the locations in which you practice.

Step 1: The initial sequence to teach your dog to whoa, or to stand, is to start from a sit position, lure your dog into a stand position, and click as she moves into position, followed by your reinforcer. Once that becomes easy, add your cue word "whoa," and slowly increase your criteria, i.e., have her stand in position for one second before you C/T, two seconds, three seconds, five seconds, and so on.

Once you reach reliability at 10 seconds, start moving small distances away from your dog, immediately returning, C/T, and so on. Adjusting to movement can be difficult, so you may need to start by simply leaning away from your dog if he wants to follow you. When moving away from your dog becomes easy, then try moving away and staying away for longer periods of time; for example, instead of taking two steps away and immediately returning, take two steps away, stay away for five seconds, and then return to your dog, C/T, and release.

When your dog can hold the position for 30 seconds while you move completely around him, start adding distractions, such as bending over to tie your shoe, making arm movements similar to lifting a gun, rustling the grass in front of the dog similar to what you'd do to flush the bird, and so on. Remember to keep training records of what you've worked on in each session (see Chapter 3), so you can build on your dog's skills in a systematic manner. Record keeping will also help you find holes in your training, show you where you may have lumped together too many steps if things don't go well, and give you some idea about how far back you have to go in your training process, if necessary.

Step 2: Repeat the same progression as in Step 1; however, start while you are walking very slowly, just a few steps at a time. When you stop, be prepared to C/T when your dog stops his forward motion. Good, loose leash walking skills will aid in your success with this step. When your dog is reliable at this skill, go ahead and add the "whoa" cue. It is important to put off adding the cue until your dog knows the behavior so that you are not training the cue during forward motion. If you keep saying the cue and your dog doesn't respond by stopping, you may be actually teaching your dog that "whoa" means "keep going"! Do a lot of starts and whoas in the beginning so you can get in many repetitions and keep your ROR high. The goal is for "whoa" to mean "stop moving and stand in place until further notice." When you and your dog are successful from a slow walk, increase and vary your walking speed between whoas. When your dog reliably stops when cued, start adding length of time to the whoa, add movement away from your dog, and so on as in Step 1, above.

Step 3: Up to this point you have been standing right next to your dog when you give the "whoa" cue, and your dog is beginning to generalize what "whoa" means. Now it's time to increase your distance from the dog when you give the cue. Here it is helpful to have an assistant who can hold your dog's leash or a check cord. Stand a few steps in front of your dog and call her to you. Just before your dog reaches the end of her leash, give the "whoa" cue. Be ready to C/T if your dog whoas on her own. If not, your dog will come to the end of the leash and you can C/T the whoa at that time, assuming she's not straining at the end of the leash. Take a few steps back and do another repetition, and so on. If your dog doesn't understand, go back and do a few whoas that she does understand and is successful at, and then try again. If you don't have an assistant, tie your check cord to a doorknob or around a tree so that you have an anchor. Slowly raise your criteria by being further and further away from your dog when you give the cue, and in different locations, such as in front, to the side, and behind.

Step 4: Now it's time to start taking it on the road, so to speak. So far we have been practicing in relatively low-distraction areas such as in the house, garage, and in the yard. Next you want to start practicing in other physical environments. Whoa is easy to practice when you are on normal walks with your dog. In fact, normal walks with your dog are a great time to practice any obedience behaviors! Start finding new locations to practice, such as a tennis court, football field, or baseball park. These are great places to start. There are new smells and distractions, but not as many as in the field environment. Even so, remember that when you change locations, you will most likely experience a regression in your dog's skills, and will have to go back

A Wasted Training Day ... Or Was It?

Mary, one of the authors, decided it was time to take the whoa skills that she and her pointer, Kate, had been working on in the house out into the backyard. The first time out that day, Mary and Kate had barely gotten started when Daisy, their other dog, started barking at a rabbit on the other side of the fence in the neighbor's yard. It was too much for Kate, and the session was over. During the next session, their neighbor Bob, who always has the best treats, came out and, once again, Kate checked out of the training session. On the third try, the neighbor kids, who Kate adores, came running over to the fence to say hello. Once again, training ended. Lessons learned? For Kate, probably not much, but Mary was reminded of some very basic training ideas:

• You can't control all the elements of your environment, but you can anticipate and plan for many things if you take some time to think it out. For example, keep the other dog in the house, select the time of the day when distractions you do or don't want are more or less likely to occur, and select a secluded area of the yard first, rather than working right in the middle.

• Don't forget your tools, such as a leash or check cord and higher value treats, in case they are necessary.

• Satiate your dog to the environment for a few minutes first, if possible (see Chapter 2).

Sometimes you just have to laugh at yourself and enjoy the learning process. Remember that you are learning, too, and when you are new at something you often miss the obvious.

a few steps in her training. The time it takes to be successful in new environments will depend on how high the new distractions are and how solidly you have trained the skills in the yard. Be sure to find situations in which you can practice whoa in the presence of other dogs. This helps to set you up for success when teaching your dog to honor another dog's point later on.

Step 5: Move your training into a more realistic field environment and essentially do the same as you did in Step 4 above.

Step 6: Once you are sure that your dog has a solid whoa, it's time to start introducing birds to the process so that finding a bird becomes the cue to whoa out in the field. Essentially this starts out as a "whoa with a distraction" exercise. First place a couple of retrieving dummies around the yard and, with your dog on a leash or check cord, walk her over to each of the dummies one at a time, and tell her to whoa when she notices it. C/T for a successful whoa, and heel her away from the dummy. Assuming she is successful, the next day repeat the exercise with a small amount of pheasant or quail scent on each of the dummies. As your dog is successful, increase the amount of scent and start hiding the dummies so that they aren't in full view, such as in longer grass or behind a piece of wood. Next, wrap the dummies in pheasant feathers or use a Dokken pheasant dummy, gradually making the training more realistic. Move on to replacing the dummies with frozen birds and then partially thawed birds. Eventually, through this process, your dog will start to whoa on the scent of the bird and the verbal cue will no longer be necessary. (Again, remember to keep good records of your training.)

If you are able to work with live birds, this is the point in your training when you would introduce them. But be cautious! If a bird flushes suddenly, that stimulus can distract your dog to the point that she ignores the "whoa" cue. That's why using a remote bird releaser that you can control is useful for this process.

Introducing Birds

Views differ as to when to introduce our dogs to birds. Many US trainers do it very early with the intent to build drive. British trainers tend to wait until basic obedience is solid and then introduce birds in a very controlled way using captive birds. Regardless of when you introduce them, do it systematically. If your dog's first exposure to birds is to have one fly up in his face, it may trigger his prey drive and he'll love it from the beginning, or it could frighten him and you'll have to add "overcome fear of birds" to your training plans! A systematic approach will help you avoid the latter.

For pointing or setting dogs, when you are ready to start adding live birds to your training, you should generally follow the same sequence you've used for all your other whoa training, only this time using live birds. You may notice an increase of intensity in your dog; she might point at the bird rather than just standing in a whoa position. Start with the bird in some kind of container, such as a cage box, so that if your dog does break from her point and successfully reaches the bird, she will only get a mouthful of wood and wire (or whatever materials your container is made of). Just as with the training dummies and the frozen and thawed birds, attempt to move the box up and down or side to side to encourage staunchness of point or holding the whoa despite bird movement. The act of releasing the bird or flushing it in front of your dog becomes part of the sequence for teaching steady to wing and shot (defined in the next section). A remote bird releaser—see Figure 8.3—can be very useful here.

8.3 Remote Bird Releaser

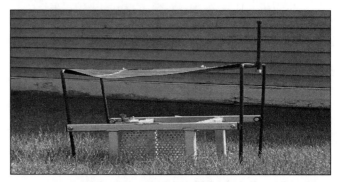

When the launcher is cocked, a pouch holds the bird until it is released upward by remote control.

Unlike pointing and setting dogs that seem to understand that charging in after a live bird will never actually result in getting one, a flushing dog seems to believe just the opposite—that charging in after the bird is what you're supposed to do! Introducing birds to flushing dogs is an extension of your quartering exercises, only you are planting live birds instead of dead ones. Some people like to "dizzy" the bird before planting it in the grass or whatever cover you plan to use. To do this, you grasp the bird around the wings and move it gently around in a circle until it gets a bit dizzy and falls asleep. Another option is to loosely tie the bird's legs together and pull some of the primary flight feathers from one of its wings. With some birds you can simply tuck the bird's head under its wing to put it to sleep. The idea is that you want the birds to stay fairly still, but lively enough to get up and fly when you get there. Using any of these techniques, some of the birds will be slow enough that your dog can actually catch a few. (In every case, after your dog has charged the bird, you will want her to sit until released to find the downed bird.)

When teaching your dog to retrieve, you introduce her to birds by systematically converting your training dummy into a bird. Start by adding bird scent to the dummy, then gradually adding feathers to the dummy—first one wing, then another, then another, and so on—until the dummy is covered with feathers. Next switch to using frozen birds. If you find that the bird's surface is too hard and your dog doesn't want to pick it up, thaw it out slightly so the surface is a little softer, or use a little duct tape to secure some air-temperature feathers around the frozen bird. Another option is to place the frozen bird in a cutoff stocking and use it that way first. Next, move on to less and less frozen versions—yesterday's frozen, today's cold but not yet thawed, and then on to completely thawed birds. Finally, switch to using freshly killed birds.

For dogs that hunt several varieties of birds, it's helpful to work them on every type they are likely to encounter, and especially birds of various sizes and weight. Retrieving a chukar is a lot different from retrieving a Canada goose!

Steady to Wing and Shot

Remaining steady to wing and shot is a skill that is common to both flushing dogs and pointing and setting dogs; however, it means something slightly different for each of them. In the US, pointing and setting dogs are expected to stay on point until the hunter flushes the bird, shoots at the bird, and releases the dog to retrieve the bird. Flushing dogs immediately drop into a sit after they've flushed the bird, until released by the hunter.

Pointing dogs

Once your dog has found and pointed on a bird, the goal is to keep your dog staunch on that point and stay there until after the hunter has flushed the bird and fired on it. This allows the dog to mark the bird when it falls to assist in the retrieve. It prevents your dog from running in and catching the bird and keeps your dog safe from being in the way of a shot on a low-flying bird. Steady to wing and shot is required if you intend to hunt test or field trial

Pointers Don't Sit ... Or Do They?

One of the longstanding beliefs among pointer trainers is that their dogs should never be taught to sit. They reason that sitting can become a "default behavior," so that the dog might sit if confused, rather than point or continue the hunt.

We have a different view. If sitting, quartering, and pointing are all under "stimulus control" (see Chapter 3), the dog should have little difficulty distinguishing the proper cue. Remember that dogs are great discriminators but poor generalizers. Consequently, it has been our experience that they can distinguish the proper behavior based on the environment and the cue given by the handler. So feel free not to teach sitting to your pointer if you wish. But if your gun dog is also a family dog, sitting on command is a useful skill in the home and, if taught carefully, is unlikely to interfere with your dog's field work.

your dog. Teaching your pointing or setting dog to be steady to wing and shot is an extension of its whoa training, but with an extremely high distraction level. Bring your dog up to a hidden dummy or frozen bird out in the field, and, once he responds to "whoa," have your assistant start to move the dummy or frozen bird a few inches crosswise in front of your dog while he is on whoa by pulling the bird on a fine rope or fishing line. C/T for a successful whoa and heel your dog away.

Repeat this a few more times. Watch your dog's body as you start to add this distraction. If he shows any sign of wanting to chase after the dummy, end the exercise and heel him away (negative punishment) before he dives after it. If you are still unsuccessful after a couple of repetitions, go back a few steps in your whoa training and build up to this again.

Once you are successful, increase difficulty by dragging the bird crosswise for longer distances, crosswise but closer to your dog, away from your dog quickly, using jerking motions, and—finally—by simulating flushes. Build even more realism by simulating the act of you flushing and firing; walk past your dog to the dummy, flush with your foot, flush by picking up the dummy and tossing it, raise a rifle up as though you are about to shoot, and so on. You may find it useful to get a remote bird releasing device (see Figure 8.3) for this phase of your training.

At this point you can also start adding gunfire to your arsenal of distractions. Your dog should be conditioned to gunfire prior to adding this step, so refer to the section on gun conditioning earlier in this chapter. When using your gun, never fire directly above your dog's head or you could damage his ears. Walk out in front of him, pretend to flush your prey, and lift and fire the gun.

Flushing dogs

While pointing and setting dogs remain in a whoa at the time of the flush and shot, flushing dogs drop into a sit position. The reasons for this difference are that the flushing dog will have already flushed up the bird for the hunter, so dropping into the sit

position gives him something tangible to do to stop the forward motion (chasing the bird), and brings his nose up out of the grass so it can mark the fall of the bird. You teach this by gradually building up the distraction level of the "sit" command to the point of pairing it with the flush so that the flush actually becomes the cue to sit.

Flushing and the Premack Principle

Pointing and flushing are tailor-made for using the Premack Principle (see Chapter 1). Recall that this principle involves using a "high probability" (desirable) behavior to reinforce a "low probability" (less desirable) behavior. To use the principle in shaping the point and flush sequence, work first on training your dog to whoa or point, as described earlier, and use the flush as a reinforcer. Most gun dogs want to chase that bird, so if you permit them to do so after responding to the whoa, then the whoa becomes much stronger. You can use a remote bird launcher, shown in Figure 8.3, to release the bird. A note of caution: do not use this method unless you are confident you can control your dog after the flush or with your whistle stop or recall cue.

Step 1: The first task is to teach your dog to sit as described in Chapter 4. You should be able to cue your dog to sit in very distracting environments and know that she will stay there for long periods of time. You should also be able to cue the sit when you are standing or walking at a distance from her and while she is moving, and still get compliance. This is similar to whoa training for pointing and setting dogs, but the behavior is "sit no matter what, no matter where, and no matter what you are doing at the time."

Step 2: Place a couple of retrieving dummies around the yard and, with your dog on a leash or check cord, walk her over to each of the dummies one at a time. As she expresses interest in a dummy, cue your sit behavior, C/T, and heel her away toward your next repetition. Start adding a small amount of pheasant or quail scent to each of the dummies. As your dog is successful, add to the amount of scent and start hiding the dummies in longer grass, behind a piece of wood, and so on, so that the dummies aren't in full view. Wrap the dummies in pheasant feathers or use a Dokken pheasant dummy to gradually make the training more realistic.

Step 3: Since the behavior you are after is to sit after the flush, not at the sight of the bird, start flushing your training dummy. It's helpful to have an assistant who can be on the other end of a fine rope or fishing line that is tied to your dummies. As your dog approaches the training dummy, have your assistant pull the dummy just a couple of inches. Cue your dog to sit, C/T, and heel her away. You will build on this by having your assistant pull the dummy farther, faster, in a more jerky manner, and so on, and by increasing the duration of your dog's sit. Start adding body movements that simulate raising the gun and firing after the "bird" has been flushed before you C/T and end the exercise. Move on to replacing the dummies with frozen birds and then partially thawed birds.

Step 4: Next have your assistant stand out farther in the field and toss the dummy a small distance up from the ground, as though the bird was actually flushed. At this point you are still standing next to your dog. Give the cue to sit after the "bird" has been flushed, then C/T. During a hunting situation you will be following your dog, not standing next to her, so as she is successful, start increasing the distance between you and your dog when the "bird" flushes. Start varying the height and distance that your "bird" is flushed. When this process is successful with you at a distance, repeat the process, but flush the "bird" closer to your dog. As before, work up to using dummies that are as realistic as possible, then frozen birds, then thawed birds, and finally live birds as you practice. Again, a remote bird releaser can be very useful.

Honoring/Backing

Honoring, or backing, is a skill unique to pointing and setting breeds. If you are out hunting with other dogs, it is impolite for your dog to barge in on another dog's point. If you want to compete in the higher levels of hunt tests or field trials, your dog will be required to have the skill of honoring when she comes upon a dog that is already on point.

First and foremost you will need to make sure that you have practiced and successfully taught your dog to whoa in the presence of other dogs, but not necessarily at the sight of dogs. When training the new skill, you want the sight of another dog on point to become the cue for your dog to whoa, and ideally, to go on point herself. Practice this out in the field with another dog that is also solid on points and is not bothered by the presence of another dog. If there are no other dogs available, you can make what is sometimes known as a "Judas Priest" dog (a term coined by trainer Paul Long), a life-sized silhouette of a dog on point cut out of a piece of plywood and mounted so that it can stand on its own. If you don't have a pattern, Paul suggests that you trace your own dog lying on its side and paint it in a pattern similar to those of other pointing or setting dogs.

Go back to working on whoa in the same fashion as before, only this time use the "whoa" cue each time you come upon your Judas Priest or your partnered working dog that has already been set on point on either a scented training dummy or a dead, frozen, or live bird. Tell your dog to "whoa," C/T, and heel it away. Over time, raise your criteria so that your dog is holding the whoa for longer periods of time. The goal is for the sight of the dog on point to become another automatic cue for your dog to whoa. In order to prevent your dog's frustration, or from learning to point only as a backup to another dog, do just a few repetitions of these at a time before allowing your dog to locate and point on a scent of his own finding.

The Complete Gun Dog

If you have diligently followed this program, you now have a gun dog that will quarter, hunt, point, honor, and retrieve, all on command. It surely will take you a long time, but the effort will be worth it. Whether your dog is a hunting companion, a test or trial competitor, or a family companion that is a joy in the field, you can both be exceedingly proud of your accomplishments. And you have achieved these results by using the most modern and humane methods available.

A Hunting We Will Go ... Or Not!

A question that often arises in discussion groups is, "When should I take my dog hunting for the first time?" Our answer is, "Not until he is ready!" Hunting is the ultimate in lumping, the stacking up of criteria involving difficult tasks and high distraction. We can't give you a precise age for the first hunt, but we do not recommend taking puppies out into the field just for experience and we do not think they can learn effectively by imitating older dogs. Rather, we recommend that you do your yard work thoroughly, work systematically by splitting your training goals, and diligently install all of the skills you will need before your first hunt. That way the first trip out will be a great success for you and your dog!

Chapter 9

The Positive Gun Dog

Success Stories

Can you train a gun dog using positive methods? You bet! Many of the methods described in this book have been proven by hunters and handlers in tests up through the Master Hunter level.

But don't you need to use at least some punishment to ensure reliable behavior in the field? Sure! We need to diminish unwanted behavior as well as improve desired behavior. But there is little need to use positive punishment (often called "correction") if the appropriate behavior is taught systematically and benign negative punishment, such as time-outs or denying the retrieve, is available.

Moreover, there is good reason to think that mixing reinforcement and punishment actually diminishes performance. Karen Pryor notes in her groundbreaking book *Don't Shoot the Dog* (Simon & Schuster, 1984) that using both can have undesirable results: "First, the accelerated learning stops, as the subject goes back to learning at the 'normal' rate: slowly. Second, if the trainer is not careful, the subject stops learning altogether—and stops wanting to learn, which is worse."

Consistent positive training can avoid these traps. And, as Pryor notes, clicker trained dogs often actually initiate training sessions with their enthusiasm. That has been our experience as well. Positive training increases energy, promotes initiative, and deepens the relationship between dog and handler in a way that force-based or mixed methods do not.

The PositiveGunDogs Yahoo Group discussion list contains dozens of anecdotes about dog/handler teams that have succeeded in the field and in hunt tests. Here are a few of them:

Jim and Toby passed their Working Certificate test in July 2005. They have continued to train and Toby is now running land and water blinds and has become a reliable and joyful hunting companion. He is also a therapy dog, working with Jim's wife Vicki as a Delta Society Pet Partner.

Our friend Tom Reese achieved a Senior Hunter title with his standard poodle, Wick, and is now running tests at the Master Hunter level. Tom is also running Junior Hunter level tests with Wick's son.

Another list member used "traditional" training drills, modified for positive methods, to reach both Senior Hunter level in AKC tests and Seasoned level in UKC tests.

The Karen Pryor Clickertraining Honor Roll lists three flat-coated retrievers, a golden, and a Labrador with Working Certificate and Junior Hunter titles, as well as two dogs—a German shorthair and a vizsla—that have achieved Master Hunter titles with clicker training. Another clicker trained vizsla was awarded both Junior and Senior Hunter titles with straight passes! Karen Pryor's list also contains dozens of dogs that have achieved other titles, from Canine Good Citizen to Schutzhund, entirely with positive methods.

But can the positively trained dog hold its own with those that are force-trained? Sara Thornton, DVM, shared this story with us:

> When I was competing Ruby, with my first Junior Hunter dog (later to become my first champion), CH Hemlock's Red Sapphire CDX JH WCI, I went to a particularly difficult trial, known to be a warm-up for field trialers. We got through the morning land marks without problems, although the word was the judge had made disparaging remarks about "show dogs." The first afternoon water mark (land, water, land) seemed particularly difficult and many dogs were quitting. I was getting very discouraged seeing people with far more experience getting dropped. My run number was close to 60. I left the gallery as I couldn't stand to watch it anymore. Finally it was our turn. We went to the line: Ruby nailed the retrieve and received a standing ovation from the gallery.

And there are many people on the list and elsewhere who are enjoying working with their dogs in the field and training them without force.

The Road Ahead

These are positive but modest accomplishments. Positive training for gun dogs is in its infancy and there are many challenges ahead for those who choose this route. But, hopefully, this book provides a foundation for further developments in positive field training and we look forward to hearing from readers about their achievements and adventures.

Gun Dog Training Resources

Classes

Basic Field Skills Class and Positive Field Training Group: Jim Barry, www.ridogguy.com

Positive Training for Hunting Dogs: Mary Emmen, www.newdoggie.com

Internet Discussion Groups

PositiveGunDogs Yahoo Group: subscribe to PositiveGunDogs@yahoogroups.com

British Gun Dog and Bird Dog Discussion Forum: www.less-stress.com/gundog

Clicker Gun Dogs, hosted by Helen Phillips: subscribe to clicker_gundog@yahoogroups.com

Books and Pamphlets

Don't Shoot the Dog!, by Karen Pryor (www.clickertraining.com)

The Culture Clash, by Jean Donaldson

Excel-erated Learning, by Pamela Reid

The Power of Positive Dog Training and *Positive Perspectives*, by Pat Miller

Clicker Gundogs, by Helen Phillips (www.clicker-training.com)

Grade One Training Manual, by The Gundog Club, UK (www.thegundogclub.co.uk)

Whoa-Train Your Dog to Performance Levels, by Steve Rafe (www.starfire-rapport.com)

Training Retrievers for Marshes and Meadows, by James Spencer

Retriever Training—Back to Basics Approach, by Robert Milner

10-Minute Retriever, by John and Amy Dahl

Hey Pup, Fetch it Up and *Retriever Pups*, by Bill Tarrant

"Broadsheets" developed by Eric Begbie, a British trainer (www.less-stress.com/gundog; Begbie also has a good online bulletin board)

How to Help Gun Dogs Train Themselves—Taking Advantage of Early Conditioned Learning, by Joan Bailey

Total Retriever Training, by Mike Lardy (Note: uses traditional methods but is a good resource on what to train)

Retrieve, by Shirley Chong (the steps to teach a retrieve available at www.shirleychong.com/keepers/retrieve.html)

Clicker Training for Obedience, by Morgan Spector (www.clickertraining.com; not hunting oriented, but a good source for info on how to train positively using a clicker)

Tri-Tronics Retriever Training, by Jim and Phyllis Dobbs (a good source of drill ideas; don't use the electronic collar)

Videos

Total Retriever Training and *Total Retriever Marking*, by Mike Lardy

ABCs of Retriever Training, by Mike Pind

Gun Dog Training Hunting Retrievers, by Kenneth Roebuck

Training and Behavior Education

Raising Canine telecourses and online courses: www.raisingcanine.com

Fun Timing Resources

Visit www.raisingcanine.com/Owners/Pink/ Owners_onlineresources.htm for the following:

Hit the Dot

Click the Chicken

Whack the Penguin

Sniffy the Virtual Rat

Gun Dog Tests and Trials

In addition to being hunting companions, gun dogs compete in tests and trials to earn titles. Many breed clubs sponsor a basic Working Certificate (WC). For a Lab to earn a WC, for example, she must retrieve shot birds on land and in the water out to about 50 yards. There are higher level tests that involve longer distances and distractions such as boats and decoys. Dogs at these levels must also do blind retrieves, delivering birds that the dog did not see fall by following whistle and hand signals from the handler.

Field trials, sponsored by the AKC, are structured events in which dogs compete against one another in tasks of increasing complexity. They often involve multiple long retrieves, distant blinds, and very heavy cover. Some gun dog trainers, dissatisfied with what they perceived as a disconnect between field trials and real hunting situations, organized hunt tests, in which dogs gain titles by performing a specific set of tasks. The tasks increase in complexity as dogs move from Junior to Senior and Master levels (or the equivalent title, depending on the organization). The AKC, the United Kennel Club, and two other organizations—North American Hunting Retriever Association (NAHRA) and North American Versatile Hunting Dog Association (NAVHDA)—offer hunt test programs. You can find details on their websites: www.akc.org, www.hrc-ukc.com, www.nahra.org, and www.navhda.org.

A Working Certificate test is a great way to check your dog's progress and meet other people who enjoy working their dogs. Hunt tests are set up to be fun events (although competitiveness is on the rise) and provide a systematic program to evaluate and set goals for your dog. They can also be addictive! Field trials are highly competitive and are intended to identify the top dogs in terms of innate hunting skills and trainability. Field champion dogs command high prices for stud and breeding.

There is a new gun dog training and evaluation program that is very promising for positively trained dogs. The United Kingdom's Gundog Club has developed a six-level test system that takes dogs systematically from a beginning level through a series of incremental steps, to more complex and demanding tasks. This is a relatively new approach, but there are two aspects that make it especially appealing for positive trainers. Details are available at http://thegundogclub.co.uk.

First, it is systematic in laying out the criteria for success and consequently fits well with the incremental approach that is inherent in clicker training. Second, it has the typical British emphasis on obedience and steadiness built in from the beginning. Thus it fits very nicely with the approach outlined in this book.

II-1 Beginner Retrievers

Beginner Retrievers: Snow, Rusty, Bentley and Brooke.

Jim, one of the authors, has structured his introductory classes and special training weekend seminars around the goals of the Gundog Club program, with good results. In the first class, five of six dogs (see Figure II-1) passed their Beginner Retriever test. The test required them to walk at heel, hold a long stay, come when called, and retrieve two dummies. All of the dogs—ranging in age from seven months to two years—succeeded after completing an eight-week positive-training program.

Training Records

You can copy the training record forms on the following pages for your own use. They include a basic training log, a behavior progress chart, and a combined form.

Training Log

\#_____   Date_____   Time_____   Treat_____

Session Goal: _____

Beginning Measurement: _____

End Measurement: _____

Summary of Session: Distance _____   Duration _____   Distraction _____

Orientation _____   Location _____

Training Log

\#_____   Date_____   Time_____   Treat_____

Session Goal: _____

Beginning Measurement: _____

End Measurement: _____

Summary of Session: Distance _____   Duration _____   Distraction _____

Orientation _____   Location _____

Training Log

\#_____   Date_____   Time_____   Treat_____

Session Goal: _____

Beginning Measurement: _____

End Measurement: _____

Summary of Session: Distance _____   Duration _____   Distraction _____

Orientation _____   Location _____

Training Log

\#_____   Date_____   Time_____   Treat_____

Session Goal: _____

Beginning Measurement: _____

End Measurement: _____

Summary of Session: Distance _____   Duration _____   Distraction _____

Orientation _____   Location _____

Behavior Progress Chart

(Proofing)

Behavior:_____

BASICS	Done	Comments
Distance		
Duration		
Distraction		
Orientation		
Speed of Compliance		
Other:		

GENERALIZING		
Living room		
Kitchen		
Bedroom		
Porch		
Front yard		
Backyard		
On leash		
Audience		
Standing		
Sitting		
Lying on floor		
Front position		
Heel position		
Back to dog		
Other		

PROOFING		
Inter-command discrimination		
Random order series		

Sample Retrieve Training Record

Training Log   Toby Retrieving: April, 2005

#_1___   Date _April 1, 2005_____   Time _6:45-7:30 AM__   Treat _Liver biscotti and happy bumpers_____

Session Goal: _Warm-up after break due to weather_____

Beginning Measurement: _Four out of five at 25 yds. in last session (March 15)_____

End Measurement: _Three sets, five trials each. First: 5/5 at 25 yds. Second: 4/5 at 35 yds. Third: 5/5 at 35 yds._

Summary of Session: Distance _25-35 yds.__   Duration _N/A____   Distraction _Many songbirds, dog droppings, one dead fish!_

Orientation _Into wind, away from sun_____   Location _Sapowet Marsh WMA_____

Training Log

#_2___   Date _April 3, 2005_____   Time _7:45-9:00 AM__   Treat _Liver biscotti and happy bumpers_____

Session Goal: _Increase distance on marks from winger_____

Beginning Measurement: _Five out of five at 35 yds. in last session (April 1)_____

End Measurement: _Three sets, five trials each. First: 2/5 at 50 yds. Second: 4/5 at 35 yds. Third: 4/5 at 50 yds._

Summary of Session: Distance _25-35 yds.__   Duration _N/A____   Distraction _Many songbirds, dog droppings, dead fish is still there!_

Orientation _Into wind, away from sun_____   Location _Sapowet Marsh WMA_____

Training Log

#_3___   Date _April 4, 2005_____   Time _5:00-5:30 PM__   Treat _Liver biscotti and happy bumpers_____

Session Goal: _Increase reliability at 50 yds_____

Beginning Measurement: _Four out of five at 50 yds. in last session (April 3)_____

End Measurement: _Two sets, five trials each. First: 4/5 at 50 yds. Second: 4/5 at 50 yds_____

Summary of Session: Distance _25-35 yds.__   Duration _N/A____   Distraction _Little wildlife (one rabbit), dog droppings_____

Orientation _Into wind, toward setting sun (masked by trees)___   Location _Simmons Mill Pond WMA_____

Combined Form

Rate of Behavior (compliance)

Session Log #: _____ Treats Left: _____ Rate: _____

Session Log #: _____ Treats Left: _____ Rate: _____

Session Log #: _____ Treats Left: _____ Rate: _____

Session Log #: _____ Treats Left: _____ Rate: _____

Session Log #: _____ Treats Left: _____ Rate: _____

Session Log #: _____ Treats Left: _____ Rate: _____

Session Log #: _____ Treats Left: _____ Rate: _____

Session Log #: _____ Treats Left: _____ Rate: _____

Latency (speed of compliance)

Session #: _____ Total: _____ / _____ = _____

Session #: _____ Total: _____ / _____ = _____

Session #: _____ Total: _____ / _____ = _____

Session #: _____ Total: _____ / _____ = _____

Session #: _____ Total: _____ / _____ = _____

Session #: _____ Total: _____ / _____ = _____

Session #: _____ Total: _____ / _____ = _____

Session #: _____ Total: _____ / _____ = _____

Speed (overall speed of behavior)

Session Log #: _____ Time Allotted: _____ Total Treats: _____ Treats Dispensed: _____

Session Log #: _____ Time Allotted: _____ Total Treats: _____ Treats Dispensed: _____

Session Log #: _____ Time Allotted: _____ Total Treats: _____ Treats Dispensed: _____

Session Log #: _____ Time Allotted: _____ Total Treats: _____ Treats Dispensed: _____

Session Log #: _____ Time Allotted: _____ Total Treats: _____ Treats Dispensed: _____

About the Authors

Jim Barry

Jim with some of the graduates of his positive field-training class.

Mary Emmen

Mary with Daisy and Kate.
(Photo by David Denney.)

Jim Barry, Certified Pet Dog Trainer (CPDT) and Certified Dog Behavior Consultant (CDBC), works out of Middletown, Rhode Island. He provides private and group instruction as well as behavior modification services throughout southern New England. Jim is an active member of the Association of Pet Dog Trainers (APDT) and edits the ethics column for the APDT newsletter. He is a member of the Head Start team at the Potter League for Animals, working with challenging shelter dogs to improve their chances of adoption. He is the only US trainer certified as an assessor for the United Kingdom's Gundog Club. Visit Jim's website at www.ridogguy.com.

Mary Emmen, MA, has been showing families how to teach their dogs to be well-mannered family members through group and private lessons and behavior consultations in the Minneapolis-St. Paul area of Minnesota for more than a decade. Mary has been active with the Animal Humane Society for almost 15 years, both as a trainer and as a volunteer in various capacities. She is also a member of the Association of Pet Dog Trainers (APDT) and actively mentors students interested in a variety of dog-training careers. Her current "pack" includes Daisy, a Llewelyn English setter, and Kate, a pointer. Visit Mary at NewDoggie, LLC; www.newdoggie.com.

About the Authors *(continued)*

Susan Smith

Sue with her first springer, JodieAnn.

Susan Smith, Certified Trainer and Consultant from the San Francisco SPCA Academy (CTC), Certified Pet Dog Trainer (CPDT), and Certified Dog Behavior Consultant (CDBC), works out of Austin, Texas. Susan does some private consultations, but her business now focuses on developing educational and business materials for trainers, consultants, and other animal professionals. She is active in her professional organizations and is chairperson for the APDT Member Relations and Communications committee. She regularly contributes articles to professional journals and newspapers. Susan studied with the renowned positive trainer Bob Bailey and with Jean Donaldson, who is one of the most respected consultants, speakers, and authors in the dog arena. Susan is co-owner (with Mary Emmen) of the PositiveGunDogs Yahoo Group discussion list. Her breed of choice is the English springer spaniel, and her canine companion and co-educator is Jimmy Joe. Visit Susan's website at www.raisingcanine.com.

532864